A Scrap Screen

A Scrap Screen

ALICE BUCHAN

The house stamps its own character on all ways of
living; I am ruled by a continuity I cannot see.
Elizabeth Bowen, *Bowenscourt*

Hamish Hamilton: *London*

First published in Great Britain 1979
by Hamish Hamilton Limited
Garden House, 57/59 Long Acre, London WC2E 9JZ

Copyright © 1979 by Alice Buchan

British Library Cataloguing in Publication Data
Buchan, Alice
    A scrap screen.
    1. England—Social life and customs—19th
    century 2. England—Social life and customs
    —20th century
    I. Title
    924.081   DA533
    ISBN 0–241–10223–5

Printed in Great Britain by
Bristol Typesetting Co. Ltd, Barton Manor, St Philips, Bristol

*To my brothers John and William,
and to the dear memory of Alastair*

Contents

Illustrations

A*

I

Lost Domains

In the nurseries of my childhood there used always to be 'scrap' screens, three leaved, the leaf nearest the child's bed being almost bald because its occupant, banished to bed while it was still daylight outside, solaced his exile by picking off the scraps. Time has given them a gloss of sentiment under a yellowing varnish, through which is seen Queen Alexandra in her wedding dress, Gordon at Khartoum, the Nevsky Prospect by moonlight, snowbound travellers being dug out by St. Bernard dogs with large concerned faces, and always children, with or without kittens, hoops, and spinning tops, ragged children without shoes, rich children in buttoned boots. Interspersed with these were Christmas cards of robins and windmills and tumbledown cottages. The glue dries, the scraps begin to peel, the child delightedly tears them off; no adult of my generation can see an ill-treated scrap screen without a small pang for what has been lost.

Scissors and paste! I can still hear the tone of humorous disparagement used in the Oxford circles in which I grew up to dismiss with these words a historical work that was not the fruit of solid research; the text being a hotch-potch of other 'serious' historians' published works, and intended, like a scrap book, to be ephemeral. Denigration was only by implication: the stuff was readable it would be admitted, and would give pleasure to readers who did not look for fresh ideas. I speak of a generation of critics now passed away who did not envisage the coming of historical 'best-sellers'.

What I am about to do would certainly have been dismissed by critics of an earlier generation as a 'scissors and paste job'. As I have come three generations late to writing about my forebears I have no choice but to draw on letters and diaries, hoping to be tolerated more readily because of the real hunger that is felt for other life-styles than our own.

The recent loss of a close companion, my mother, the loss of an intelligence that had been uncompromising in its beliefs though prepared to be convinced of new ways of thinking, laid on me the weary necessity of going through family papers alone, deciding which to keep and what to destroy. Leafing through diaries bound in shiny black canvas with marbled endpapers was a sadder task than reading letters which still conveyed the small impulse of energy that caused them to be written. Diaries make the most depressing reading, the *cri de coeur* if it breaks through is immediately smothered, and the slow ticking of a time-clock (a clock that in these old diaries was always slow) like a heavy heart makes itself heard.

I am an amateur and write for pleasure. I have learnt no tricks of the biographer's trade. I can only offer this in extenuation, that though the people I am going to write about caused no great stir in history, they lived within the limitations of a social structure sending up their branches and sinking their roots deeply in the certainty of the survival of their world. They were, as I shall hope to show, the inheritors of the virtue of seemly behaviour, a virtue we, today, appear to have mislaid.

I am writing this at the time of year when grass is bleached and leaves show their undersides; the fatigued interim of late summer before September with its reviving richness sets one thinking of new clothes and garden projects. I feel like the season, a nondescript. The child of late Victorian parents, I took longer than most children to piece out an identity for myself, rooting myself in other children's nurseries, in family houses in the country (I was myself a London child), in housekeepers' rooms, potting sheds, pantries; conveyed about, blinkered, of no fixed period in time.

Let it not be thought that I am making out a case for a deprived childhood. I was born of an amazingly happy marriage, with grandmothers, great-aunts and uncles and innumerable cousins, all living in large family houses in which it was possible to leave a book with a page turned down in a bookshelf and find it there undisturbed when one returned months later to finish it. Good places to read were the broad-seated old W.Cs, or the deep cushioned window-seats, or the back stairs. Children were left alone by servants who had their own work to get through. Thus I read all of Henty, Seton Merriman, Stanley Weyman, Rider Haggard. This was how I grew to be observant and to make myself unnoticeable, trying as far as possible to avoid the dooms of childhood—being sent out 'to play' and 'make friends' with other hated children when I would rather be reading. The other side of the baize door spelt literary enfranchisement for me, a fact that would have surprised my elders.

If these lines come into the hands of someone who has felt as I do for the lost domains of childhood, let me bring to memory the sour smell of silver polish in the pantry and the special smell of the brick used for knife grinding; the scrubbed soap smell of uncarpeted nursery stairs rising over a well up which, from the kitchens below, floated intimations of what was being cooked for the dining room (but not for the nursery); the indescribable wet warm scent of greenhouses full of forced carnations, azaleas, gloxinias, waiting to fill the gilt baskets in the drawing room; and those drawing rooms, richly scented with pot-pourri made from the petals of the first red roses of summer, never the pink or white, mingled with the lemon tang of China tea, what a snare to the unwary they were, with their polished parquets! A trip over a shoe-lace could turn into a slide and a clutch at a small table loaded with an oil lamp and myriad fragile objects (I was seldom not in disgrace for clumsiness).

Servants, one's refuge and comfort, were never absolutely to be trusted, they had to keep on the right side of their employers, cheat a little, keep a sharp eye out; that they could be selfless, discreet, devoted, has been eloquently testified (they could as easily be lying, greedy, two-faced). To children cooks were invariably cross because of their feet, gardeners morose, butlers often kind and most approachable when occupied by some calming chore like cleaning silver. The last debts—duty visits from the children they bullied, and betrayed—were gladly paid. Through small chinks of memory slide some we never saw like the Log Boy, whose duty it was to watch an hourglass run through and at the last grain hurry to carry logs to where the footman kept the log-baskets for replenishing the downstairs fires, and the Spider Boy, who had a bunch of feathers tied to a long stick for knocking down spiders' webs on the grounds that they ate holes in the carpets. All these must have ceased to be on the wage-roll long before I was old enough to notice, for households were shrinking; no longer did a Major Domo remove yesterday's used blotting-paper from writing tables before housemaids had a chance to hold it up to a mirror and read what indiscretions had been penned the night before. In retrospect servants, a vanished race, are voices in the next room, shadows seen through a half-open night-nursery door, dipping and elongating in the fire-light. They were a limb from which the life-blood has seeped away. One thing is very sure, without them that particular way of life can never come again.

The denigrated sentiment of nostalgia—in Greek meaning pain for a lost home[1]—feeds on reconstructions of the *vie de château*, but it is poor fare. Half a loaf may be better than no bread, but it does not satisfy so well.

Houses in public ownership can go no more than halfway to meet the visitor. It takes a disciplined and informed imagination to picture a dinner party from which the last human vibration has long expired, even though the evidence is all there—the damask table-napkins, the candelabra, the wine-coasters, the finger-bowls, and all the labour-making paraphernalia that we are so glad to be rid of. Over the glitter of glass and gold plate the air does not move, feeling is not stirred.

Dispossession diminishes. Passing down an enfilade of rooms furnished at the happiest period of English design, striped with sunlight from south-facing windows—rooms by whose now empty hearths lovers once looked into each other's eyes, then threw down books and embroidery frames to catch hands and run out into the sunshine—we are faced by what has been irretrievably stolen from us: a life style. Regret for something not known is deepened by a sense of our having been some time, somehow, fobbed off by life.

Some of the tin boxes that are ranged round my desk are crammed to overflowing with title deeds, wills, catalogues of sales of land, of furniture and pictures (these last are saddest reading of all). From where I sit to write, surrounded by all these, I hear an outside clock striking the quarter hours on a cracked note, reminding me of Landor's words—'the present like a note in music is nothing save as it appertains to the past and what is to come'.

What lies in front of me is a task that appals: of recapturing from the evidence of these boxes the life-styles of my forebears and to attempt to give life to the surroundings in which I grew up.

Writers write in order to be noticed, to make their voices heard above the crowd; amateurs like myself sometimes never get past that initial impetus. I believe that all writers, even the professionals experience a strong disinclination to bridge the yawning void

[1] A form of melancholy caused by prolonged absence from one's home or country. *Shorter Oxford Dictionary*.

between beginning and non-beginning. There is something the opposite of inviting about a piece of virgin foolscap.

I look round me and think how lucky it is for me that the room I write in is furnished without what is known as taste, with valueless or unplaceable pieces turned out of rooms viewed by the public. (This house,[2] my husband's family's, has been a property of the National Trust since 1946.) Coming together like this the furnishings make no demand on one, offer no suggestions, hint no criticism. There is an 1822 pianoforte such as Beethoven could have composed on, sofa-tables by Gillow of Liverpool, a fire-screen with a coat of arms embroidered within an innocent wreath of honeysuckle, red and gold Japanese Imari plates, lacquer boxes full of mother-of-pearl counters for Loo and Spadille, a Buhl teapot, its compartments lined with silver paper for Green and Gunpowder tea, a Minton bust of Shakespeare, a Bath Gainsborough, a reputed—but not by the experts admitted—Poussin.

Grateful for the room's indifference to me (I could not impose myself on it if I would) I try idly (procrastinating) to count the objects in daily use, all of them worn by much handling, that have survived to be part of the pattern of our living, and that will continue to be so. Take the fire-screen : a fragile useless object, devised to keep the heat of the fire from delicate complexions. This leads inevitably to the position in the room of a fire-*place,* defended by a *fender,* an object invented to fend off sparks from the hearth rug. There will be *arm*chairs with arms at a convenient height to rest the elbows when reading a newspaper, *foot*stools for lifting thinly-shod feet away from draughts, and so on. This physical approach to the past has its sentimental side and likes to think of domestic objects still filling a need, of cups, candlesticks, spoons, pokers, shutters, cushions, foot-stools, still being used for the purposes for which they evolved, the design never having been bettered. It would be rash to attempt to define aesthetic taste which has filled the dustbins of history with pieces of matter looking a little more used and battered each time the dustbins are emptied. This room would, I fear, have been dismissed by my great-aunts as chiefly housing bric-à-brac, several of its contents would have been banished to the servants' bedrooms without argument. They had their own standards, conditioned by inheritance, travel, education.

[2] Charlecote in Warwickshire.

With Morris wallpaper and de Morgan tiles, my own grand-parents felt that they were proclaiming the virtues of the 'simple life', when in fact they knew nothing about simplicity of the sort they aimed for. The next generation were of 'the Sargent-Furse era', of glassy chintzes, and buttery portraits. The Second World War brought reaction from the white satin sofas of the '30s, and 'taste' has now veered back to the stripped pine and rush matting which were the legacy of the Arts and Crafts movement, when ladies in Passionate Brompton hung their walls with blue and white Japanese plates. Researchers of the future will find it hard to pin a name to an era as nerveless as the one we are living through.

In the tin boxes lie evidence of more than a century of tastes and attitudes that could not be considered nerveless or ordinary; of an eighteenth century *dilettante* architect who was also a bishop, of thinkers, writers, hostesses, wits, beauties and many kind comfortable people. The choice of where to begin is baffling.

One of the boxes, the weightiest, contained books, a motley lot that had been salvaged from an auction, broken-backed, damp-spotted. From the sermons, medical dictionaries, and battered copies of Baedeker's guides to the Cathedrals of Europe, emerged three volumes bound in crushed calf that had once been handsome. The life of Lady Mary Wortley Montagu by her grandson, who was my great-great-grandfather.[3]

Witty in an age that valued wit above the virtues, Lady Mary crossed swords verbally with Pope, who came off worst. She loved and married a mean, cold man whom her warmth could not melt, Edward Wortley Montagu, had one daughter who happily returned her love and a worthless son who broke her heart. Wounded, she was able to avoid being bitter; lonely, to be proud.

'Human nature,' she laid down, 'without any additional misfortune furnishes disagreeable meditations enough. Life itself, to be supportable, should not be considered too near.' I can almost hear her adding to me, 'Take your characters as you find them, yet judge as kindly as you can.' She had a mordant wit, but through harsh experience learnt to rein it. She said humbly of herself after being accused of having uttered a hasty judgement, 'perhaps I have been indiscreet, I came young to the hurry of the world.'

[3] James Archibald Stuart Wortley.

I think back to a portrait of her recently seen in a picture-
dealer's in St James's. Though considered a beauty in her time we
should admire with more reserve the protuberant heavy-lidded eyes
and the full lower lip that betokens sensual appreciation of the
good things of life, but also a desire to put the world to rights,
which in one way she did for she introduced inoculation for small-
pox into England. Her advice that one should pluck up spirit and
live upon cordials when one can have no other nourishment, I have
always followed.

Well, there she is on one side, my maternal grandmother's; on
the other side, my never known maternal grandfather's, were the
Grosvenors whom it is hard to love, too well-dowered with the
world's gifts to be intriguing, but virtuous, high-minded, dismally
respectable (those of whom I write); and the Wellesleys, mercurial,
caustic, suspicious, stubborn. A mixed inheritance, but traces of
these virtues and foibles are in all my generation, and, I must
suppose, in myself, though one hopes for a preponderance of the
foibles.

In the pocket of a blotter lined with white moiré silk I find two
envelopes so broadly bordered with black that the sender (Queen
Victoria) could barely find room for her flowing hand to set down
the recipient's name—the Honourable and Very Reverend Gerald
Wellesley, Dean of Windsor. He and his sister Charlotte (who
was my great-grandmother) were the children of Sir Henry
Wellesley, Wellington's elder brother, and his wife, Lady Charlotte
Cadogan, who ran away from her husband with the Marquess of
Anglesey and whom Sir Henry had to divorce. It was a *cause
célèbre* that rocked even the Regent's London.

The children of Henry Wellesley who suffered most from the
scandal lived long lives of blameless respectability. Gerald went
into the Church, lived to be Dean of Windsor, and become the
valued support of the Queen in her widowhood. Charlotte married
my great-grandfather Robert Grosvenor, and lived far enough into
the nineteenth century to be still held in living memory. I have a
watercolour drawing of her in old age, her fine hands curved
round a large tea-cup—containing the weak China tea she preferred, known as Grosvenor Wash—her star-sapphire eyes still
bright; she had been telling a grand-daughter (who did the sketch)
how, as a girl and when her father was ambassador in Vienna, she
had ridden in the park of Schönbrunn with Napoleon's son who

bore the empty titles of King of Rome and Duc de Reichstadt.

Her favourite daughter-in-law was my mother's mother, Caroline Stuart Wortley, her youngest son Norman's wife. Caroline's grandparents had inherited and improved a house, Wortley Hall near Sheffield, built on a much older foundation. Their architect had been John Platt of Rotherham. The next generation to inherit it built on to it, but discreetly, using local stone the colour of Sheffield's smoke-filled skies. This plain four-square house contented five subsequent generations. It now has the stranded appearance of a house through which a consecutive stream of life no longer flows.[4] Under Victoria it was enlarged with a tower and an achievement of arms on the pediment soon to be etched in black by the smoke of Sheffield's collieries—the 'Sheffield blight' of which Sir George Sitwell of Renishaw in the same Riding refused to admit the existence.

My mother's father's home to which Caroline came as a bride, Moor Park in Hertfordshire, was, in startling contrast, a white Palladian palace. The Venetian painter Amiconi frescoed the hall with classical scenes, Capability Brown transformed the dullish piece of Hertfordshire in which it stands into a very fair imitation of Italy. With lavish use of Prussian Blue and Chinese White my grandmother has captured the play of indigo shadows across the house's façade of Portland stone. The Italian garden was formal and spiked with cypresses; the Wilderness was a tangle, as its name implied, of wild fruit-trees, their branches interlacing to make a flowery ceiling; azaleas spread, liking the soil, in all the permutations from faintest rose to blood-red. An inspired sense of order set flights of steps and statues and graceful balustrading wherever convenience required them, and decreed the placing of water and flower borders to lend sentiment to formality and ravishment to the eyes.

The Grosvenors were Whigs, (the Yorkshire Wortleys were Tories) and because the Whigs virtually ruled England under the Georges and had great riches and political power as well as an unquestioning assurance that history was on their side, it was almost a categorical imperative that the day-to-day living in a high-minded Whig household should be carefully unostentatious. At Moor Park meals were served with ceremony though food eaten off green

[4] In 1948 it was sold to the Rotherham Labour Party and is now a rest home and conference centre for members of the party.

Sèvres china was only good by nursery standards. Charlotte Wellesley, my great-grandmother, who married Robert Grosvenor, was once mistaken for a beggar when she went paying calls on foot, and once, because she dressed so shabbily, was sent down to the Servants' Hall. When she went to visit the poor in the village, and whatever the weather, she walked. At Wortley great fires of Silkstone coal from the Wortley collieries flamed up all the chimneys. Moor Park, partly because of Charlotte's obsession with fresh air, was so cold that the sons and daughters of the house huddled in one sitting-room. Charlotte gasped for air, feeling smothered by the not excessive (by the standards of the time) luxury of Moor Park. She endured it with private prayer and self-denial. My grandmother, using the greater freedom of self-expression of her generation, got away. My mother was determined not to let it imprison *her*.

By that time the life of the greater country houses was slowing down, based as it was on undeviating routine carried out by unmurmuring servants drawn from the villages round about and educated for domestic service and nothing else in schools built by the squirearchy. (The village schools are closing now, the churches in the parks are being declared redundant, as for the cottages more than half of them are dark all the week till the week-enders arrive.)

After 1918, when foundations were cracking in all directions, Moor Park was sold for a fraction of its value. The Chinese wallpapers went, the Adam sophas and fauteuils crossed the Atlantic, but the Amiconi frescoes were not movable. A golf course now replaces Capability's landscaping of the park.

The poet of our time[5] who has most lovingly and perceptively chronicled our age has written:

> Did ever golf club have a nineteenth hole
> So sumptuous as this?
> Did ever golf club have so fine a hall?
> Venetian decor, 1732.
> And yonder dome is not a dome at all
> But painted in the semblance of a dome.
> The sculptured figures all are done in paint
> That lean towards us with so rapt a look—
> How skilfully the artist takes us in.

[5] *Metroland* by Sir John Betjeman, Poet Laureate.

What Georgian wit classic Gods have heard,
Who now must listen to the golfer's tale
Of holes in one, and how I missed that putt,
Hooked at the seventh, sliced across the tenth,
But ended on the seventeenth all square.

Ye gods, ye gods, how comical we are!
Would Jove have been appointed Captain here?
See how exclusive thy Estate, Moor Park.

An odd sequence of ownership, yet inevitable once Metroland crept up to its borders. I sometimes think how pleasant it must have been to live in early Metroland; how pleasant to take that green suburban train from Baker Street to Chorley Wood to return in a Spring dusk to a house with lit windows, Liberty linen curtains not yet drawn, and to know that all around there would be other houses, identical, half-timbered, pebble dashed, standing in thickets of rhododendrons; guardians of family life and advanced taste, and warm as Moor Park in its stately isolation never was!

Looking back across the gulf of years—and perhaps no greater gulf has ever existed between generations—I see with a child's eye a genial gloss on my elders, a ruddy glisten of satisfaction with their lot. They were always going out shooting or coming in from hunting bringing with them the frosty air and the red sunset. Walter Bagehot wrote: 'It did not matter that Squire Western spent his nights under the table if he spent his days in the open air'—and it was this open-air flush on them, and the ease and good temper that went with it, that made the tireless pursuit of sport by landowners entrenched among acres that retained their early feudal boundaries, so poetic.

Having quiet minds that leaned to moderation in all things, they inclined to be tolerant of the world that clamoured beyond their confines. But in those quiet minds there was germinating through the nineteenth century and into the twentieth an unease that made them redouble their benevolence to the weak and unfortunate, so that they balanced their pleasures with strenuous charity. The houses they inherited are perhaps finer than their owners, on whom the light of a declining day sheds a not altogether deserved glow.

So the scraps from coloured 'supplements', scissored by an unsteady childish hand, fragments of snowy parks, autumnal woods, village churches with their windows lit for Evensong, are pasted

on the screen making a rich impasto of the charge of the Scots
Greys at Waterloo, Disraeli in profile, and Finden's large-eyed
beauties, without relevance yet with some eye to effect. My name-
sake, Lewis Carroll's Alice, another Oxford child, possessed a
stern commonsense that armed her against being taken by surprise
on her journey through the Looking Glass. Once and once only
did she relax to indulge the kind of sentiment that I myself confess to. The White Knight, archetype of all fussy misguided
grown-ups was never to fade from her mind; 'Years afterwards she
could bring the whole scene back again as if it had been yesterday—
the mild blue eyes and kindly smile of the Knight, the setting sun
gleaming through his hair and shining on his armour in a blaze of
light that quite dazzled her—the horse moving quietly about with
the reins hanging loose on its neck, cropping the grass at her feet—
all this she took in like a picture . . .'

2

Ancestors: The Earl Bishop and his Granddaughter

As I have said, I was a solitary child, never alone (with three brothers) but of a turn of mind that sought solitude for private enjoyment. Houses were my first books, with their smells and echoes, and sensations to the touch of smooth and rough, heat and cold. I can still feel the chill that struck up from the black and white marble floor of the hall of 30 Upper Grosvenor Street, the house in which my mother's mother lived. She had been a Stuart Wortley from Yorkshire and had married a Grosvenor, and No. 30 was a Grosvenor grace-and-favour house, now obliterated since it stood close to old Grosvenor House and suffered the same fate.

The staircase curved slightly but gracefully up to two drawing-rooms on the first floor, a small one looking over the Grosvenor House gardens with its tall sycamores, and a large front-room looking onto the (then) quiet street of houses that were all replicas of the same excellent ordered design, through blinds made of amber and blue Venetian beads strung on silk cords. Both rooms were papered with the Morris willow-leaf paper. We were hardly ever allowed in the front drawing-room as the floor was said, on what authority I do not know, to be unsafe, which added, for a child, to its mystery. The back drawing-room was consequently densely crowded with furniture, and hung with photographs and water-colours, and plates of beautiful dim purples and greens which I now know to have been Persian and of great value. There were also a number of low, buttoned chairs onto which one's elders obligingly crowded to witness plays written and acted by the children of the family; the heavy velvet curtains that divided this room from the mysteriously unsafe front drawing-room made a natural stage. From the windows you looked on the tops of trees; you could have been in the country. Among the photographs on the leafy wallpaper was one that I liked to return to, and have explained to me. One of my grandmother's sisters who, having had no children of her own, took a cool interest in me, was ready to do this.

The photograph was a family picture then hanging in her father's old home, Wortley in Wensleydale, depicting a breakfast party in lodgings at a Swiss Spa in 1786. Evian-les-Bains was a pleasant, not smart, resort to which minor foreign royalty and the dowdier English nobility went for the medicinal baths. Here had come my great-great-great-grandmother, Lady Erne, and her sister-in-law, Lady Hervey, with their two little girls who were very near in age to each other. On this occasion their guests were a royal couple, the Prince and Princess of Piedmont, she the sister of Louis XVI whose dreadful fate though still some years away was coming toward him at that moment.

The obliging great-aunt liked to dwell on the ladies' dresses— *pour marcher à la campagne*—one of them being *feuille morte* silk accompanied by a hat trimmed with huge loops of amber silk ribbon. (They could not, I thought, surely have been meaning to go for country walks dressed like *that*.) Breakfast in that context did not mean what the word meant to me, I thought poorly of the rolls and honey provided. What delighted me was the stout tabby in the foreground, its back turned on the company. I christened the picture 'the unsnobbish cat'.

All the life of the scene, which as a painting is rather stilted and dull,[1] seemed to me to be centred on one of the two little girls: Caroline Creighton who was to be my great-great-grandmother. I would *think* myself into the picture; sisterless, I thought how much I would like to have her to play with. Two great-greats seemed to put us at an untraversable distance (yet I now reflect that my own mother, so recently gone, was my own granddaughters' great-grandmother and at once the gap narrows. In relationships frontiers are arbitrarily placed).

The Piedmonts conceived a great affection for their hostesses. In 1789 when Lady Erne and her daughter were on their way home through France to England the Princess wrote to her *Chère Milady* begging her from the depths *'d'un coeur triste et affligé'* to visit the Princess's sister Madame Elizabeth on her way through Paris and send news of her. Lady Erne, though an invalid, did not lack courage, and she braved (with Caroline) the spitting blue-chinned

---

[1] The original by Guttenbrünn is still in the possession of the present Earl of Wharncliffe. It was a gift to Lady Erne from the Princess.

Republican Guards at the gates of the Tuileries in order to carry out this tragic last request.

I identified much later from a family inventory the dark blue and gold breakfast china, the black Wedgwood teapot and milk jug, the silver urn, for Lady Erne travelled with her own household gear. But as a child my interest was all for Lady Erne's little daughter, who in the painting is waiting to hand the cup that her mother is filling with cream, good manners concealing the impatience little girls feel towards their mothers. She grew up with warm colouring, dark chestnut hair, widely spaced dark eyes, and her famous aunt Elizabeth Foster's delicious *nez retroussé*, which moved the historian Gibbon to say that she, Lady Elizabeth, had only to beckon for the Chancellor to leave the Woolsack for her.

I choose the date 1803 for an event of no political importance that took place in it (and, one must admit, of little private importance either), the death in Italy of Frederick Augustus Hervey, Bishop of Derry in Ireland and fourth Earl of Bristol, with whom this chronicle of family history begins.

It was not an uneventful year since it saw the rupture of the peace of Amiens, negotiated in order to give Britain a breathing space in the war with France. It was only a paper peace, and not expected to last. Gunshot hissed, as waves tossed against the wooden sides of British ships in the Mediterranean and off the coast of Holland. During the 'peace' the massing at Boulogne of Napoleon's gunboats could be ignored. Two years earlier, at Marengo and Hohenlinden, he had annihilated the strength of Austria, thereby getting control of the Austrian Netherlands and bringing his armies uncomfortably close to the shores of England. However, while briefly at peace with France it was possible for the English to forget the Dutch batteries, which were after all a good way off from the Essex port of Harwich. National confidence in the might and resourcefulness of Britain's navy was boundless, and two years later to be confirmed by the victory of Trafalgar. The loss of the Earl Bishop was regretted by few people, certainly not by his wife and children. He was a figure from an earlier age, larger than life-size. Only the eighteenth century could have given him the scope his grandiose ideas required.

Such characters are the product of their times and the accident of their birth. Frederick, born in the middle of the eighteenth century, was one of the eight children of John, Lord Hervey of Ickworth, and an Irish beauty, Molly Lepel, Lady-in-waiting to George II's Queen; a man equally loved and feared. 'If you call a dog Hervey I shall love him,' Dr Johnson said, and plain but far from stupid Queen Caroline so doted on Lord Hervey that she was heard to say, 'It is well that I am old or I should be talked of for this creature'. Pope poured vitriol on Hervey's sexual ambivalence, his personal vanity (he dieted and tight-laced to keep his figure and painted his face to hide the ravages of time and ill-health). His impudent wit, his bland indifference to public opinion, were handed on to his third son Frederick Augustus. The looks of Molly Lepel skipped a generation to reappear in the Bishop's second daughter Elizabeth, who seduced and married a Duke of Devonshire.

On leaving Cambridge Frederick Augustus took Orders, chiefly to pacify his wife[2] who feared the strain of inherited levity in his character and with good reason. Possibly she thought that the Church would have a sobering effect on him. It was the only resource for a younger son without inheritance who was not attracted by the Army or the Law, and provided a position encumbered by only a minimum of religious observance which allowed free scope for the development of gentlemanly interests, such as coursing hares, teaching tame birds to talk, botanising, playing the flute, and in Frederick's case the study of geology and the natural sciences. Interest in engineering was edging him in the direction of becoming a self-taught architect.

On being invested with the Bishopric of Cloyne in county Cork through the influence of the Viceroy, his brother the 3rd Earl, he set about draining the Great Bog of Cloyne. He has been called an eccentric, which in his dress—outrageous for a Bishop—he was, yet many of his actions were both practical and benevolent such as the draining of Cloyne—for the Bog was stagnant and agriculturally unproductive. Next he threw himself with passion (in all his involvements, and there were many, often on behalf of others, he was passionate) into improving the lot of the poor Catholic clergy of his diocese who lived no better than their beasts. Religious in any sense other than simply orthodox he was not, but he loathed injustice. Aristocratic English pluralists holding Irish benefices which they never visited, on the livings of which they battened

---

[2] Elizabeth Davers, daughter of Sir Jermyn Davers, Bt.

(having acquired them for purposes quite other than pastoral), resolved him never to appoint an Englishman to any benefice of his. He was not troubled by the bugbear of consistency; his own position as an Irish Bishop who was also an English Earl was questionable, but it would not have occurred to him to recall the fact, or if he recalled it to allow it to deter him.

The influence he hoped to leave behind him was purely aesthetic. He said of himself: '*Pour moi, j'irai mon train,* and if I cannot be the Caesar or the Cicero, I will be the less splendid but a more useful citizen, the Lucullus of my time, the Midwife of Talents, Industry and the hidden virtues.' He was to enjoy one sort of fame. His demon of energy which in the end shortened his life, kept him endlessly on his travels to Europe. He was the type of English Milord who was most dear to the heart of foreign inn-keepers, and he permitted certain hostelries where comfort was assured to be named after him. As the nineteenth century went on, more and more Hotels Bristol appeared all over the Continent, and in most capital cities (there to this day), so that in one sense the Bishop was prophetic in congratulating himself on being the Midwife of the Hotel Industry and promoting the hidden virtues of clean linen and hot water.

The more valuable See of Derry succeeded Cloyne, and with it the emergence of what was to be the devouring interest of his life: building. He has been loosely called an eccentric but this I cannot accept. The Oxford Dictionary definition of the word is 'regulated by no central control, irregular, anomalous, capricious', which comes near to his character but not near enough. He was clever, excessively selfish, greedy, vain; the axis round which he pivoted was himself. Life for him was to be a hall of mirrors endlessly duplicating his own figure posturing in a variety of disguises to suit the mood of the moment. He genuinely believed his tastes to be simple, daylight and champagne were all he demanded. The child of Pope's 'Sporus'—

> Amphibious thing, that acting either part,
> The trifling head or the corrupted heart,
> Fop at the toilet, flatterer at the board,
> Now trips a lady, and now struts a lord . . .

could hardly be ordinary. His violent and often capricious temper he inherited from his Irish mother. Frederick Hervey started life poor and a third son in an age and a society that adored wealth, noble birth, and personal beauty. His appearance was meagre, his vanity enormous. He meant to have nothing less to reflect his mirror image than the greatest works of the greatest masters in a setting reminiscent of classical antiquity. Alberti, Palladio, and Vitruvius were to be his inspiration. He appropriated to himself a piece of land within his diocese of Derry, Downhill on the cliffs of Antrim, and there began his first experiment in building. Intoxicated by the possibilities presented through his researches, which were scholarly and thorough, into engineering and archaeology, he went on to build another classic Folly, Ballyscullion on the shore of Lough Beg. He was by now the fourth Earl of Bristol, and the possessor of a fortune. He comes within the scope of this book with the birth in 1779 of his first granddaughter, Caroline Mary Creighton; the little girl with dark hair cut *à la Jeanne d'Arc* in the painting by Guttenbrünn of the Evian breakfast party.

The Herveys had had bad luck with their children, three having died in infancy. Their two elder daughters, Mary and Elizabeth, married very young and were bad choosers. Mary married a widower, John, 1st Earl Erne, who already had five children and had not, it seems, much need for another wife, except as a step-mother for them. Elizabeth married, before she was eighteen, an Irish landlord, John Foster of Dunlear, bore him two sons, endured his morose temper for four years and left him. The Ernes (it is more difficult to know why *they* did not get on) agreed to live apart, coming together occasionally for Caroline's sake.

The Herveys were embarrassed by their father; their mother's life with him had been tempestuous to begin with and in the end, wretched. On a carriage drive during which they quarrelled, the Earl Bishop had flung at her some detail of his private life which caused her never to speak to or see him again. Quarrels they had had before in plenty, and poor Lady Bristol must have been well inured to being told that, with her narrow Puritanical ideas, she was incapable of appreciating her husband's tastes, but this was something so wounding, so shocking, that it made up her mind to leave him forever (she had her own small fortune).

The Bishop was understandably annoyed that the girls had made such stupid marriages and been so comparatively unfruitful. When in her grass-widowhood Elizabeth Foster became *ami de la maison* at Devonshire House and the mother of two children by the Duke, the Bishop perhaps did not care to be reminded that he had written to her in the early days of her first marriage: 'Go on, my dear Eliza, and never fear hurting your constitution by honest child-bearing.' He did not live long enough to see her become the Duke's second Duchess.

Mary Erne was delicate and the Bishop hated people to be ill; anyone's ill health but his own bored him. But he loved his grand-daughter, little Caroline Creighton, his Lal-Lal as he called her, and intended that she should be the prop and comfort of his old age.

Lord Erne was not generous to his estranged wife, and Lady Erne and Caroline owed the small comforts of their lives to the Bishop's infrequent spasms of fatherly feeling. When they were living in lodgings in Lyons, he wrote to Mary from Bath: 'If it be practicable, I wish to pick up such a little drab as you at Lyons before the cold makes the transit of the Alps too hazardous for your poor shattered frame. When you are tired of kissing Caroline for your own sake give her One for mine. You have time yet to send me commissions—the Time and my purse will bear it.'

Thus Mary was to winter in Italy with Caroline, aged seven but forward for her age. In October 1785 he wrote from France that he awaited the arrival of his horses from England before proceed-ing '*avec des bottes de Sept Lieues—ou de Quatre Jambes, qui nous vaillent bien*'. He intended to visit an old friend in Lyons—'You must allow me one day with Madame le B., which tho' a Sabbath will *not* be a day of rest. Yet no holding up of little Fingers, Madame Mary, *nous ne sommes pas sur ce pied là*, ours is all Platonism, Sentiment and Politicks—fuel more suitable for 55 and a constitution lacerated by unintelligible disorders and unintelligent physicians.'

The winter in Italy and the medicinal baths at Evian did do Lady Erne good. She and her little daughter returned to Italy, spent the spring and summer of '87 in Rome and moved from there to Florence. Naples which the Earl Bishop loved she thought un-wholesome and she feared another eruption of Vesuvius. I have been unable to follow their wanderings since there are no family letters until 1789 when they set their faces homewards, visiting in Paris the Family of France in virtual imprisonment in the Tuileries, implored to do so by the heartbroken Princess of Piedmont. Lady Bristol was nearly out of her mind at the thought of these two beloved creatures being exposed the horrors of revolutionary France. She felt it necessary to point a moral lesson to Caroline, aged ten—'you are entering into life at an awful moment, but I hope the miseries of other countries will teach you to love your own and revere that national character which, now putting aside all animosity and private interest, makes a firm and generous unanimity the impenetrable bulwark of our happy constitution'.

The Earl Bishop's concern for his delicate daughter was too erratic to be depended on. The South coast of England was salubrious and cheap and there the mother and daughter took lodgings. It was there that Mary Erne heard of the execution of Marie Antoinette. 'I am stunned,' she wrote to her sister, 'by the deplorable End of that most Unfortunate Woman. Her whom I have seen at the very Summit of Power, of Happiness and Glory, surrounded by adoring Crowds, to whom her smile was fortune, joy, and too secure delight. And, dearest Louisa, how can one think on the reverse!'

The death of their eldest brother brought the three sisters—Mary, Elizabeth and Louisa—closer, and to be near them and their mother Lady Erne decided to settle with Caroline in London. Caroline was her mother's chief concern and joy; it seems to me that she was, as well as pretty, a sensible child, cheerful and practical too. She did not allow time to hang on her hands but read a great deal, and worked at her drawing. She was to complete the design for a frieze at Ickworth left unfinished at the death of the designer, Flaxman. She designed her own clothes and bonnets, which often had to be retrimmed to make them appear new.

In a family chronicle love and marriage cannot be held off for long. Caroline's fate was coming towards her. By now, Louisa Hervey, the Bishop's youngest daughter, had married Robert Jenkinson, a rising young MP, whose father, who had held Parliamentary office under Lord Bute, was still living and had recently been ennobled as Lord Liverpool. Louisa, now Lady Hawkesbury, took Caroline under her wing. Better than the rosy colouring and pretty hair was Caroline's natural cheerfulness and readiness to be amused. Whatever people might say about the Bishop, no one could deny that he was always alert for new experiences and enjoyed everything that came his way, a more useful trait to have handed on to one than mere beauty. She had through her aunt,

Elizabeth Foster, the *entrée* to Devonshire House, hardly a decorous background for a young girl, but it was difficult for Lady Erne to refuse her own sister's invitations, equally difficult to seem to condone a *ménage-à-trois* with the resultant 'children of the mist'.[3] Caroline Creighton and precocious imps like Caroline Ponsonby,[4] contrived a private secret-sharing existence outside which the life 'at once gorgeous and dishevelled, frivolous and tragic . . . quickened by that delicious emotional stir found only in societies whose chief concern is love' went on.[5] Hannah More wrote that London parties were no longer in the style of comfortable exclusive intimacy, but she was a tiresome prig, no one but a prig would write: 'everything is great and vast and late and magnificent and Dull'.

London can never have been more restful to the eye, a city of pale-coloured palaces, and also of red or yellow brick country houses standing back behind high walls, shaded with fresh leaves. As I write it comes back to me that this is how I must have seen Devonshire House when I was a very small child, almost rustic in its simplicity, behind a plain wall broken only by two gates, and that was how it must have looked to Caroline and her contemporaries. 'Devonshire House, that yellow brick Venetian villa with the stone facings and vases, its spacious forecourt and plain stout wooden doors (the wrought-iron gates from Chiswick House had not yet been re-erected here) exhibited a certain nonchalant grandeur, as of one who brings the country to town, and refuses to bend to the conventions.'[6]

Caroline's personal London would have been an acreage of great houses, with big gardens and muddy lanes between, overhung with trees. The contiguous area was an extraordinary patchwork of small parcels of land, fields and plots, which changed hands all the time. Following the Restoration a usurer called Hugh Audley who had grown extremely rich on advancing money to younger sons and country landowners rendered penniless by sequestration of their estates under the Commonwealth, died and left to his nephew,

---

[3] A euphemism for illegitimate, being an abbreviation of 'mystery', though there was no ambiguity about the children's parentage.
[4] Daughter of the 3rd Earl of Bessborough, niece of Georgiana Devonshire.
[5] *The Young Melbourne* by Lord David Cecil.
[6] Sir Osbert Sitwell, *The Scarlet Tree*.

John Davies, a bankrupt broker who had served a sentence in the Fleet prison for extortion, the Manor of Ebury lying on and around the marshes of Pimlico. With Audley's money Davies bought up Millbank, bordering the river, also the fields and plots surrounding Buckingham House—the house that was later to be rebuilt by George IV as a royal palace. Davies' daughter Mary, the heiress to all this, was sold at eight years of age to the Hon. Charles Berkeley, but his father being unable to pay up his part of the contract she was married at the age of twelve to Sir Thomas Grosvenor, of Eaton, Cheshire, whose grandfather had been speculating in London property with remarkable foresight since the beginning of the century. Large as her fortune was, his was as great. During Caroline's lifetime there were beginning to be built the handsome squares and terraces of Belgravia and Pimlico, named for the courtesy titles of the Westminster family.[7]

William Kent designed Grosvenor Square on the fringe of Tyburnia which was to make the West End of London fashionable. The country however is not so easily dispossessed. Kent, in his layout for Grosvenor Square, intended it to be a place for elegant strolling along neatly-ruled gravel paths; in fact its present day layout is much more like his first idea. In Caroline's day it was a thicket with in the middle of it a dairy where you could take your jug to be filled from the cow; on a bench there was still carved as late as the 1860s the words 'Louisa Wortley I love. Lovaine'.

The Wortleys had bought a house on the south side of Grosvenor Square. They were a Yorkshire family, owning steel and iron works in Sheffield. The vulgar prejudice against marrying into 'trade' was not yet beginning to find expression as it did later in the century when the rising shop-keeping class was gaining the *entrée* everywhere, to the chagrin and annoyance of the established upper classes. Coal mines were respectable to own, steel and iron no less so.

The Wortleys' son, James, was often Caroline's partner in quadrilles and at those delectable river picnics at Chiswick and Kew given by the Devonshires. She and James's sister Louisa were best friends and wrote long screeds to each other when forced to be parted. Louisa considered, and her parents agreed, that it would

[7] The two rogues, Audley and Davies, are perpetuated in North and South Audley Street and Davies Street.

be the happiest thing in the world if James and Caroline were to marry.

Louisa, who one is glad to know married her Lovaine,[8] was writing to her dear friend Creighton in August of 1797 to try to tempt her to visit Wharncliffe Lodge, the Wortley family's country retreat near Sheffield, to hear the larks singing above a ceiling of interlacing greenery.

The young Wortleys had a drawback—at least in their own eyes. They were descended from the most famous of all female letter-writers, Lady Mary Wortley Montagu, and were apt to be mortified when reminded of their great-grandmother's fluency with her pen.

'I never could give an account to be understood of anything or any place in my life, and therefore cannot attempt to describe Wharncliffe,' Louisa begins in advance, warning her friend to expect no flights of elegant hyperbole. 'Yes, I will try a little, and leave you to understand it as you can. You love *Anticaglia* (antique) houses, but perhaps you do not approve of *shabby* Anti-caglias, and I am sorry to say that Wharncliffe Lodge is rather so, being extremely little, and the *furniture*, as you have seen by my patterns (samples) having no other recommendation but its antiquity. We have but one room for breakfast, dinner, supper, hung with the lovely tapestry of which you have a piece in your possession, one couch and such a one! the poor thing is an hundred years old, I do believe, and carved and twisted about till the legs resemble a corkscrew more than anything else—we can however boast of four modern chairs. The Bedrooms are hung with blue and green Harrateen, and one with what has once been red damask. There are a pair of most curious Jack Boots which I have routed out and which I would give anything for you to see as you are worthy of them, indeed I never laugh or do anything pleasant that I do not wish for my dearest Lady Caroline.'

Remembering the necessity to make Wharncliffe sound beguiling to her sweet friend, she plays down its wild and craggy aspect. '. . . there are fine nooks and corners to *nestle* in among the rocks which Mary[9] and I resort to almost every day after dinner, and lay and stretch our limbs in the most perfect state of *dolce far niente*, while I groan out "Oh, I wish poor dear old Creighton was here."

[8] Lord Lovaine, eldest son of the Earl of Beverley, succeeded a cousin as 5th Duke of Northumberland.
[9] Married in 1813 to William Dundas MP.

In short, to conclude this *clear entertaining intelligible* description, Mama desires me to tell you that the country around is really very beautiful and puts her very much in mind of Spa, she wishes you and Lady Erne were here; among other reasons because she says you would have taste enough to admire the country. So much for Wharncliffe'.

James Stuart Wortley[10] and Caroline Creighton had been attracted at first sight. They had to wait for two years, while he completed his military training. Parvenus might be eager to have a daughter marry an historic name, but serious parents to whom social advancement was no consideration were extremely careful in the choice of sons-in-law. Religion, politics, reputation, a Place in the County, together with the question of settlements on the younger children of the marriage, all would be under scrutiny before consent was given, and one is aware that this balancing up, though it broke some young hearts, led to many wonderfully happy marriages.

The Earl Bishop was predictably cynical about marriage; he despaired when he heard his son was about to make a love match— ''Tis so ruinous a lottery, so pregnant with blanks, so improbable a success.' James and Caroline did not think so. Up till now Caroline's chief concern had been for her mother, forced to live on the charity of relations and the careless kindnesses shown by her father. Ever since she could remember, Caroline had been trying to cheer her mother up. From an early age she had bumped about the Continent in stage-coaches from Spa to Spa and known life in shabby genteel lodgings, between bouts of running wild in Ireland on her father's estate with the barefoot children of grooms, or spending sober holidays at Ickworth with her grandmother Lady Bristol who taught her to read. If she and the other child in the Guttenbrünn painting, her dear cousin Eliza Hervey, when staying at Downhill with their grandfather the Bishop, made grottoes of shells, it was too often for Caroline to have to leave hers unfinished in order to set out once more for a foreign Spa in search of health for Lady Erne.

In this way she grew up. 'Only' children, if they are daughters, come early to an independent habit of mind. If her 'onlyness' had given her a taste for personal privacy she loyally put it aside and

[10] Colonel James Archibald Stuart Wortley, aged 22, son of the Hon. James Stuart Wortley, son of the Prime Minister, Lord Bute.

B

prepared to find the not especially subtle humour of a large family as delightfully witty as they appeared to find her.

Her letters to Lady Erne are never forced, or literary (a weakness of some of her contemporaries), for she was the most truthful creature, humble about her looks and talents, always ready to be amused, to learn, to admire, to admit herself wrong. Harriet, Lady Granville, who was the daughter of Georgiana Devonshire and had no love for her mother's supplanter, Caroline's aunt Elizabeth Foster,[11] capitulated to her. In a letter to her sister, Lady Morpeth, Lady Granville wrote: 'Lady Caroline Wortley is to me like a moonlight night after a hot day, refreshment and repose. She has all the charm of intelligence without the tax of *ésprit*, is always ready to do everything, which completely captivates me. There is a charm about her one can hardly account for, but it is, I believe, perfect naturalness, great refinement, and no wish to be anything but what she is. She is entirely without the ungovernable wish to be *un peu plus* than one is, which spoils so many.'

Of all the wifely virtues good nature surely must rank high. Caroline wrote to Lady Erne in 1799 after her marriage in the March of that year: 'I assure you I am quite another creature, and instead of setting my heart on things and allowing myself to be disappointed and discomposed, I keep myself constantly prepared for anything that may happen—& even the furnishing of my house, which at another time I should have been wild about, I do with great coolness merely as an occupation—in short as long as I am allowed to accompany my husband wherever he goes, I shall make an excellent soldier's wife—but I don't pretend to being a Spartan lady when he is sent away from me.' He was not however to be sent away from her, in all their years of marriage they were hardly ever parted.

On her first married Christmas Day she wrote to her mother— 'This is a most worthy Xmas day—as cold as cold can be. Think of my forgetting that the sacrament is administered in all churches— I really felt quite vex'd, as from wandering from place to place for some time past, I have been so seldom to church and thought so little on such subjects that I could not bring myself to take it without preparation, when I heard of it for the first time this morning. I am the more vex'd because my dear Zac[12] would not take it with-

[11] After Georgiana's death to become the fifth Duchess of Devonshire.
[12] One of the many pet names for her husband.

out me, the first time after marriage—he, God knows, needs no preparation for if there is an angel upon earth certainly it is him . . .' adding a gloomy postscript, 'I wish you may succeed in your soup shops, but the poor are so provoking that one never knows what will please them'.

It had been confusing to have a grandfather who was a Protestant Bishop yet owned palaces and was a *gourmet* and covered himself with diamonds (the Bible's teaching was surely against the owning of great possessions?). With relief she found that she had married a man who was extreme in nothing but his devotion to herself, who thought the Bishop something of a ridiculous bore, who laughed at her jokes and only became serious and glum on the subject of sport. She called him by a variety of *petits noms*, Zac, The Dog, The Doge—occasionally the Vile Dog, when he stayed out too late shooting on the moors round Wortley. They lived together with mutual tenderness and reciprocal amusement for forty years.

In 1800, when Caroline was expecting her first baby, James Stuart Wortley left her behind in London to accompany his father on a visit to Yorkshire. It was the first time he had set eyes on his Yorkshire inheritance. The September sun was warm, and never had the bronzing oaks of Wharncliffe Chase looked more glorious. James came to it with the eye of ownership; earlier in the year an aged great-uncle had died, brother to the Lord Bute who was so inefficient a Prime Minister—and through this death James's father had come into the possession of a property in Scotland. James being the eldest Stuart Wortley male of the next generation, his elder brother having died three years before, his father proposed to settle on him the Wortley estates that had descended to him from Lady Mary Pierrepoint's marriage to Edward Wortley Montagu. In view of the expected child, it had been suggested that the young Wortleys should buy a pleasant villa residence somewhere near London, but, in the flush of coming into his kingdom, James scouted the idea.

He wrote to his angel: 'Well, my Dearest Dear Car, here I am actually upon the land of my inheritance and am perfectly in raptures with this lodge; my father and all the family are not at all worthy of possessing such a romantick and beautiful place *to think to getting a villa for the summer months near London*! It really surpasses all my ideas of it so that I shall say no more, but keep it

till I can give you the account by word of mouth. In the meantime
I send you a copy of the inscription upon a stone here, as it is kept
here on a dirty piece of old paper.[13] The stone lies as flooring to a
small scullery off the kitchen, and the inscription is writ in distinct
black letter characters. The old house-keeper here is the finest old
creature you ever saw, she has been in this family since my great-
great-grandfather's time[14] and calls herself 87, but she *must* be
more as she perfectly recollects Lady Mary Wortley's being married, which was in the year 1712.[15] My father and I went to pay
her a visit in her room last night, and she gave us all the anecdotes
of my forefathers with great spirit.

'I am now looking from the window down the Precipice
clothed with all variety of wood upon the finest view you almost
ever saw. No country can possibly be wilder or more beautiful, in
short the sum of all is that I am surprised and delighted . . . I am
so completely *en air* and agog that I find it quite impossible to
write or sit still for a moment—you know me so well as not to be
surprised at it. So I shall leave it off for today. God in heaven bless
you, my sweetest own dear love, take care of yourself and love me
as heartily and sincerely as you are adored by your most affect. but
most agog—J.A.S.W.'

Caroline, tenderly sympathetic, was prepared to declare the view
over Wharncliffe Chase far finer than ever Horace Walpole had
thought it. Her happiness was to grow and expand to embrace four
children, John, Charles, James, Caroline and two little girls who
died early. They moved to Wortley in the early months of 1802,
having had the fun and satisfaction of rearranging the house to
suit themselves, while staying in the small, cold, uncomfortable but
indubitably romantic Lodge. Caroline imported her pianoforte,
'which nobody can find the key of, and the poor harp which stands
in a corner in its case because I dare not attempt stringing it on
account of the extreme damp, but when we have constant and
larger fires perhaps I may venture'.

[13] A sixteenth century parchment, now destroyed, which set out the
legend of a Sir Thomas Wortley who survived being the servant of four
kings, and kept his head on his shoulders, the last of them being Henry
VIII ('whose faults God pardon'). This Sir Thomas 'caused a loge
(lodge) to be made on this crag in the mydys (middle) of Wancliffe for
his pleasure to hear the harts bel.'
[14] Hardly possible—James had muddled his 'greats'.
[15] Lady Mary spent her honeymoon at the Lodge.

Wortley—their *stammschloss*—was to be a plain house with a terraced garden, and after the cold of Wharncliffe Lodge Caroline was determined that it should be adequately heated. She wrote happily to Lady Erne: 'I am too busy with all that is going on to wish to stir . . . Pray tell dear Fred (her uncle) with my love to him, that Zac and I are reading Paley's Evidence of Christianity together, which he gave me, and that Zac is as much delighted with it as I was when first I read it—we read four chapters in the Bible every Sunday evening. He is trying to make me like Ossian, but I am still a goth upon that subject—tho' I like it rather better than I did, and shall go thro' with it for the sake of good subjects for drawing.'

Wortley, August 8th, 1802 (after the birth in London of Charles, her second child):

'Here we are once more, dearest mama, at home and it feels so natural to me to find myself in the little Library again that I can hardly believe I have been away, much less that I now have *two* children in the nursery. Our meal was soon ended, for we were dying to get out before dark and look about us—you cannot conceive how altered and improved everything is—the terrace all green with a great many flowers, the round before the house quite smooth and the circle in the middle quite green also—the greenhouse all glazed and my little room ready plaistered for papering.' The letters breathe the pleasantness of days spent in the open air and evenings in the library when they are too sleepy to write, or attempt to read Ossian, and too content with each other to care who knows it. Nagged by conscience, they compose a joint letter to Lady Erne, Zac beginning it: 'Caroline is so sleepy and so stupid that I have been obliged to snatch this out of her hand to tell you so. Now I am neither very much awake or uncommonly witty tonight, so that you are not likely to have a very brilliant specimen of our abilities in this epistle. However, there is one old stupid remark that we are sure you will like at any rate, which is that John and Charles (but particularly the first, as you know) are the ugliest and least entertaining of children. She desires me to say, too, that I am gone quite distracted about farming, that I have kept her waiting for her dinner today till half past six, having been out to look over a famous farm in the neighbourhood, that I do nothing but admire two certain models of a South Down Ram and Ewe which are arrived this evening, and talk of a living specimen of

this same species now in one of the fields, interspersed with little
episodes on patent harrows, ploughs, chaff-cutting machines etc . . .'
at which Car in her turn snatches the letter from him and con-
cludes: 'I think you are very lucky that I should have had a stupid
fit upon me, since it has procured you so *witty* an epistle from that
most impertinent reptile. I certainly never in my life felt so little
able to answer a long letter as I do tonight and am absolutely
forced to send this as it is, having barely strength sufficient to hold
my pen as you may see—so good night. The Dog is six and twenty
this day! how old!!!!!'

James had been returned in July 1802 (for the second time), as
member for Bossinney, a Bute property in North Cornwall with two
farms on it and nine electors which returned two members to
Parliament. He therefore was obliged to tear himself away from
his garden and his young family and spend part of the summer in
his parents' house in Grosvenor Square in order to attend the
House of Commons. He wrote to Caroline in May 1803, when the
Peace of Amiens was about to be dissolved, describing the debate
on Britain's renewed declaration of war with France.

Lord Hawkesbury, husband of Louisa, Lady Erne's sister, later
to be Lord Liverpool, and Prime Minister, spoke for two hours till
his voice was quite gone and the House could barely hear the
Bastard's exhortation from Shakespeare's King John with which
the speech ended. 'Then Mr Pitt got up and delivered what even
those who have heard him often say was the finest speech he ever
delivered . . . Of course the House was all attention to *him*, and
when he sat down, after he had finished his speech, the House
almost unanimously cried out, Hear him, Hear him, three times—
the same thing in short as three distinct claps in a theatre . . . The
words came from him as easily as if he were reading instead of
speaking, and every word in its right place, and the best that could
be chosen to convey the sense and make the phrases harmonious.'

The Irish crisis of that year,[16] one of those recurring revolutionary fevers of which the body of Ireland has been always subject,
terrified Caroline who was half Irish by blood. As usual the snake

---

[16] Robert Emmett, an Irish patriot, hoped to rally the diminishing band
of United Irish Loyalists and with help from France rouse his fellow
countrymen to rebel against the authority of the English Parliament. The
help from France was not forthcoming and he was arrested and executed
in 1803. His death was the inspiration of many ballads.

was scotched, not killed. She wrote miserably to Lady Erne: 'I
cannot bear to look at my babes. So far I am from thinking they
will see better times that I fancy the troubles of the world increas-
ing. I am very superstitious, if you chuse to call it so, and have for
some time past felt almost persuaded that we are several hundred
years nearer to the end of the world than is imagined, and as the
principal sign of those times is to be troubles all over the face of
the earth, I think we cannot have a more striking resemblance than
at the present time, and I look forward to no more peace on earth.'
She had to admit that the spirit of the British once roused was
impressive and her intuition, which she called superstition, 'is in
this instance a comfort to me for I feel a sort of inward confidence
that Providence will never allow that *monster* (Bonaparte) and his
crew to vanquish or even hurt this country which, however im-
perfect, is certainly the best of the nations now existing. Odious
Russia! and how made! Adieu dearest Mama. I will go to my
husband who is laying out the poultry yard, and turn my thoughts
from public affairs to private, if I *can*.'

It was not easy to be cheerful just then, though no one would
have admitted to being unduly alarmed about invasion. James
Stuart Wortley, from a firm sense of obligation to his inheritance,
attended loyal dinners and Volunteer rallies and generally lived up
to what the county expected of him. He was to become Member
for York in 1818.

To Lady Erne in the July of 1803 came the news that her father
had died in Italy. She by now was renting an apartment in Hamp-
ton Court procured for her through the influence of her sister
Louisa; it was dark and pokey but she had improved it with white
paint.

The Bishop had called her his favourite daughter, tried to
sweeten her solitary condition by giving her a coach and horses,
sent kisses and presents innumerable to his little Lal-Lal—but he
had made poor Lady Bristol wretched and this his daughters were
never able to forgive.

By the time Frederick Augustus was in his mid sixties, well
preserved, stouter, thinner about the hair, he was permanently
domiciled in Naples, making himself conspicuous by riding in an
open carriage with two mistresses, dressed in a purple soutane with
a splangled sash and a huge white felt hat. His family can only

have prayed that he would remain in Italy for ever, but there were still the two Palladian villas in Ireland, Downhill and Ballyscullion, to be completed, for which he had been prodigally buying pictures, marbles, chimney-pieces, scagliola columns, and issuing mandates for planting shrubs on the rocks at Downhill, where sixty acres of barren moor had been grassed and sprinkled with white clover. Like an outcrop of native rock on the windy cliffs of Derry ruined Downhill broods with the angry sea at its back, and the sea winds now blow through its empty walls, unhindered.

At Ballyscullion on the shores of Lough Beg, he planned to have an elliptical rotunda connected with pavilions by curving, closed-in colonnades.[17] This would give scope for the statues which he meant to set in niches all round the oval hall. The pavilions would house his collection of pictures. His daughters were the recipients of a great many letters on the subject, but no longer did the Bishop send love and kisses to his granddaughter, he had ceased to show any interest in his descendants; even Catholic diocesan reform was waning on him. Building was all.

Ickworth was to come next and to be his abiding monument. *'Mais où entrain mon astre errant?'* he would declaim rhetorically, knowing very well that his devouring curiosity would impel him in any direction where something exciting was taking place, a revolution, an entertainment, or a sale at which he might procure additions to his collection of paintings and marbles.

A contemporary of the Bishop's in America, Thomas Jefferson, one of the founding fathers of the Republic, who was also a gardener, a mathematician, a designer and an engineer, had built himself the house he christened Monticello, 'the little mountain', using, as Frederick Augustus did, the *Four Books of Architecture* by Palladio, taking ideas from them, but, being likewise of an experimental turn of mind, rejecting, altering, and revising as he went along. The British Parliament was frantically debating the war of the American Colonies but the Bishop did not trouble himself to attend the debates, being far more pleasurably occupied. That Thomas Jefferson, a dastardly, to the Bishop's way of thinking, revolutionary, lived at Monticello in the style of an English feudal landowner, with all the graces of music, books, good wine, and elegant furniture on the best English pattern that the Bishop

[17] As later at Ickworth.

considered absolutely indispensable to health and good living, would have astonished him had he known of it.

The manner of the Earl Bishop's death verged on the farcical. He was travelling to Rome by way of Albano when he was seized by cramping stomach pains, most probably acute peritonitis. The inn-keeper of the inn to which his servants carried him was a Catholic and indignantly refused to give shelter to a dying Protestant cleric. So died the man who had given his name to so many inns and hostelries. The inflated legend of his excesses went out on a gasp of breath in a dirty stable. His body was robbed of all the money he carried with him and even of its rich clothing by his servants, who then ran off and left him.

His funeral was impressive; a number of poor artists and sculptors who had good reason to be grateful for his patronage attended as well as many others who were famous and successful. The prayers of Cardinals wafted his soul to Heaven. His last public appearances had been unbelievable; in Naples he rode about in a loose bedgown and a purple velvet cap with a gold tassel, his face grown thin and sharp like a witch, giving himself the airs of an Adonis, blowing kisses to the women in the crowd. To meet his Italian debts almost all his pictures and statuary had to be sold, some simply vanished. His architectural extravagances, Downhill, Ballyscullion were like soap bubbles doomed to break. Ickworth is his immortality, the last expression of the Classical Ideal in which he flattered himself he had achieved the Pure and Noble in a manner which was to unite Magnificence with Convenience, Simplicity with Dignity.

Even after death he had to cut a caper. In order not to kindle the superstitious terror of the ship's crew on the man-o'-war which was to take his body back to England, it had to travel in a box labelled 'antique statue', and thus disguised came to Ickworth which he never saw completed.

His descendants finished the half-built house according to its original plans, and there he hangs, painted by Madame Vigée le Brun, who perhaps loved him, with Vesuvius smoking in the background—fair, fat and happily smiling, perfectly pleased with himself.

B*

3

Charlotte

Charlotte Arbuthnot Wellesley was my great-grandmother on my grandfather's side, nearer to me by a generation and also because I have been told stories of her by those who clearly remember her. Born in about 1807 (even this is in doubt) she died in 1891 in my own mother's lifetime. She has slipped through a chink of family history (as she would probably have wished to do) leaving very little evidence of herself. Beneath a photograph of her in old age are the words, embossed on the frame in silver, *'in caelo quies'*, which I like to interpret as meaning *released and refreshed*, since she longed for identification with the wind and the sky, a longing that caused her to throw open every window and sleep in a bedroom that was a 'temple of the winds'.[1] Of my forebears she was by far the most interesting and is the hardest to understand; to try to do so one must look at the circumstances of her childhood.

Almost her first memory was of driving all night (surely two nights and a day?) across Europe in a carriage with her father, and of being stopped at a frontier where there was a loud hubbub of voices in no language the child had ever before heard spoken. Long journeys were exhausting enough for grown-ups but agony for children since a coach allowed no space for small legs, suffering with pins and needles, to thrash in. During the business of changing post horses, coachman and postilions walked up and down, beating themselves to get the blood running again in their stiff limbs. There was something terrifying in the way the new horses would be lashed to a gallop to cover as much ground as possible while they were still fresh, the coach rolling and tipping till the chess pieces rattled on the travelling chess-board. Telling this to a granddaughter, (who told it to me), Charlotte, by then an old woman, was uncertain. There had been a journey, by night, and they were going, she thought, to some Congress or other—

[1] Moor Park had once an actual Temple of the Winds in its Pleasance, now demolished, upon which Dr Johnson wrote some verses.

Vienna?, but no, that was another occasion—could it have been Spain?

It was Spain, in 1810, to which her father, Sir Henry Wellesley, had been appointed Ambassador. She had been only three years old at the time and the recollection had got mixed up with other later memories of the ambassadorial years in Vienna.

Henry Wellesley was the youngest of the triumvirate of Wellesley brothers, overshadowed if not entirely eclipsed by his eldest brother, Richard the Marquis, and the next brother, Arthur, later the Duke. A shadow lay over his children too. When Charlotte was only three she and her brothers, all under six, were playing alone at the top of a big silent house in Curzon Street, when without any reason being given they were hurried away to a house in Putney, which at least had a garden for them to play in but beyond the gates of which they were not allowed to venture. They had been aware, since children are never unaware of family tensions, of their mother being often in tears and of their father's face turned from her, clouded with anxiety or stiffened in anger. Henry's French sister-in-law, wife of the Marquis, thought all the Wellesleys were inept with women (her own husband notably excepted), particularly Henry. If the Earl Bishop's daughters were bad choosers of husbands, the Wellesley men were not cut out to please wives.

Henry and his next brother Gerald, who had taken Holy Orders, married two sisters, the Ladies Charlotte and Emily Cadogan, described as nice friendly girls with plenty of 'go' to them but not much in the way of looks. One imagines that Henry was a difficult man to refuse, he had the monumental Wellesley handsomeness (they all made imposing marble busts). He was expected to have a distinguished career in diplomacy, as in fact he did. From first setting eyes on her he was attracted by Charlotte's vivacity.

Charlotte, after bearing him four children—one of whom, Gerald,[2] he later disclaimed—took a lover, by no means her first. Her sister Emily had done the same, finding life in the Deanery at Durham with the Hon. and Rev. Gerald Wellesley insupportably dull. The striking feature of the otherwise commonplace story of aristocratic adultery that follows is that Charlotte's lover, Henry Paget, created Marquis of Anglesey for gallantry at Waterloo,

[2] Who was to become Dean of Windsor.

was also a co-respondent in the Dean's divorce from Lady Emily. Henry Paget was decidedly not inept with women.

It was Charlotte's habit to walk her dog in the Green Park by way of Half Moon Street, then not much more than a lane, with a scatter of cottages along one side and the high wall of a private garden on the other, leading to the thoroughfare of Piccadilly where it was not wise to be seen lingering in masculine company. It was safer, however, than walking the dog in Berkeley Square over which the windows of her relations' houses kept frowning watch. Here, in Half Moon Lane, she and Henry Paget met and from here they were conveyed by hired cab to borrowed rooms in Mount St. They were inevitably seen. The scandal that broke on London overnight in late August 1808 (the affair had been going on since early in the year) rocked Society, shocked that a Wellesley could be cuckolded so publicly.

Henry Wellesley, of whom it was said that he was the kindest natured of the four brothers, would on very little persuasion have forgiven his wife. He was obliged to take her back in to his house in Curzon Street (from which the children had been removed) when she turned up on the doorstep, penniless, and pregnant with Paget's child, (Paget having been sent abroad on the Walcheren expedition). The reports from Putney were that the children, particularly small Charlotte not yet two, were frantic with misery at being parted from their mother. It would have been too cruel to keep them apart, so the two youngest were allowed to return to their home.

Wellesley attitudes hardened; this fuss, this publicity, was intolerable. Henry came in for much censure for having taken the *maudite sorcière* back under his roof. Charlotte was described very unfairly as a 'stinking polecat' and a 'damn nefarious hell-hound', though many people were disposed to be sympathetic to her for having preferred dashing Henry Paget to a Wellesley replica in marble. Arthur, later the Duke of Wellington, was adamant. He was himself partial to amorous dalliance on the side but believed in keeping all that sort of thing strictly *sub rosa*. Paget was a useful soldier, the divorce must go through and the whole business be forgotten as quickly as possible.

There was another aspect of the affair; Paget was in process of divorcing his own wife by the slow and cumbrous processes of Scotch law in order for her to marry her lover, the Duke of Argyll.

Kind Kitty Wellesley[3] adopted Charlotte's youngest son Gerald, 'the miserable little being' whose utter unwantedness touched her motherly heart, and for six years had him in her care. The Pagets were married in 1810, the Argylls in the same year. Lady Bessborough wrote, 'Lord Paget's children are all in town on their way from Inverary to Beaudesert; they talk with filial tenderness of Mama Argyll and Mama Paget; *Vive la Liberté*!'

Henry's two elder boys, Henry and William, were sent to their grim grandmother, Lady Mornington in Ireland to be educated; little Charlotte was the one chosen to stay with her father and in 1811 or 12 was travelling with him to Madrid, where he was to be ambassador for thirteen years.

The eldest Wellesley brother, Richard, then Lord Wellesley, was appointed Governor of the Indian territories in 1798, where an angry situation smouldered between the most powerful of the Indian rulers, Tippoo Sahib of Mysore and the Nizam of Hyderabad. With the characteristic Wellesley mixture of high-handedness, far-sightedness and bonhomie he established a lasting settlement, outbidding a French overture of alliance with the Indian princes and making them pay for the privilege of being defended against each other by the British. Henry had gone out with him as secretary and was now left with the ceded territory of Oudh to govern it as best he might,[4] Richard returning home to feud with the East India Board which as soon as he had left the country reversed most of his policies.

Henry picked up a germ in India which affected his liver and inclined him to take a gloomy view. Richard's was a nature that could ride out a storm, his was not. Not that he lacked courage, moral or physical. At the time of his divorce from Charlotte Cadogan it made him wretched to think the scandal might have harmed his brother Arthur's career. In fact the only time that Wellington ever mentioned it in public was when someone re-

[3] Later Duchess of Wellington.
[4] Richard Wellesley's vision of a united British India was in a fair way to come true by the beginning of the nineteenth century, and had he not been the loser in a wrangle with the East India Company which controlled the country's trade, an administration could have been set up there that would have avoided the blood bath of the Mutiny. Henry's gift was for diplomacy, and his share of the Wellesley tenacity enabled him to govern Oudh for two years without bloodshed.

marked that Lord Anglesey's appointment to be second in command of the cavalry in the coming confrontation with Napoleon in
Belgium might cause talk on account of his seduction of Lord
Wellington's sister-in-law; Lord Anglesey had had a reputation for
'running away'. Wellington's grim rejoinder was: 'I'll take care
he don't run away with me, I don't care about anybody else.'

The very little time I know for certain about my great-grandmother begins with the journey across Europe to Spain. After that
I have to piece the story together from scraps. Henry remarried;
his second wife was Georgiana Cecil, sister of the first Marquis of
Salisbury, who could be counted on to do what was right by
Charlotte's children and to put his career in diplomacy above all
other considerations.

But Lady Georgiana, who soon had a child of her own, was not
prepared to take on a step-daughter with such an inflammable
heredity, so until she was in her teens Charlotte lived in England
and Ireland and shared governesses with the daughters of her
step-mother's friends. She was going to be good-looking in a way
that gave her relations some alarm. At the earliest possible moment
she must be safely married off.

At seventeen she was placed under close chaperonage and
allowed by way of Hunt balls and County Assemblies to venture
into the marriage market by which an already interrelated aristocracy further entrenched itself. I possess a miniature of her done
at about this time that has faded but shows that her curls were fair
to reddish. She was tiny, very slight and an elegant dancer. Her
looks were, as the French say, *journalière*, when unhappy she could
look pinched and disapproving. I think of a granddaughter of
hers, one of the great beauties of her time, whose charm lay in
warmth of manner, an appealing glance, a joyful laugh like a
blackbird's song, and wonder if these might also have been
Charlotte's had they not in her case been tinctured by the bitter
unhappiness of her childhood.

She went out to Vienna, till now thought too dangerously
frivolous for a young girl of her antecedents, in 1828 at the age of
about twenty-one. She did not care for sitting about in the drawing-
rooms of diplomatic wives, but took long walks accompanied only
by a maid, studied German, and rode every day in the Vienna
woods. Narrow-waisted and upright, she looked well on a horse. As
daughter of the British Ambassador it was not thought unsuitable

for her to accompany Napoleon's son, now no longer King of Rome but Duc de Reichstadt in his Austrian mother's right, on the rides prescribed for his health, accompanied by grooms and aides as decreed by the boy's tutor, Count Dietrichstein. He was four years younger than she was, living a sequestered life in apartments in Schönbrunn, poring over military histories, dedicating himself to the day when he should succeed his father as Emperor of the French. Bonapartist conspiracies to oust the shaky Bourbon, Louis XVIII, from the throne of France, were kept from coming to his ears but could not be altogether suppressed. Tubercular, he lived in a febrile futile dream of kingship. Hindsight presents us with this strange pair, the consumptive boy who would not live another four years and the English girl who was Wellington's niece, riding together through Spring woods, he pouring out his obsession with war and strategy, she replying in careful schoolgirl German, her thoughts miles away with the man she had fallen headlong in love with.

Charlotte did not make friends easily, often repelling kindly-meant overtures with a coldness much at variance with her real nature. No girl of seventeen was ever more unready to resist the first man to take a warm personal interest in her. My own grandmother, her daughter-in-law, once obscurely remarked to me '*Never marry a Paget*', adding a few moments later '*nor an Esterhazy*', though I hasten to add that the opportunity to do either never arose.

Though family legend had it that she had a disastrous love affair out in Vienna no names were ever mentioned. He could have been the brother or nephew of the Prince Esterhazy who was Austrian Ambassador in London, Henry Wellesley's opposite number. But one must be wary of conjecture. Charlotte's tears (to him so like her mother's) ploughed another furrow in her father's already corrugated brow, since clearly the lover did not aspire to be, or was inadmissible as, a son-in-law. Henry Wellesley was now Lord Cowley. Charlotte must not be allowed to squander herself, she was the daughter of a rising diplomat whose career was everything to him, it was her duty to redress her mother's folly. So it was put to her by her Uncle Arthur, who bent his formidable frown on her and said 'Damn you, Charlotte, do your duty.' When as a child I was told this story, I hated the Great Duke for being so inhuman to young love.

Young men from England came and went, for Vienna was

enticing if the dull Wellesley household was not. Charlotte's greatest friend in England, Olivia de Ros,[5] who was to become her sister-in-law, often said what fun it would be when they were both married, but Olivia was a jolly unaffected creature who saw good in everyone, even in the younger Henry Wellesley whom she married, who was a dry stick like his father with the additional disadvantage of a stammer.[6]

One finds from time to time in contemporary *mémoires* references to staying with the Cowleys in Vienna, but not in such terms as makes it seem likely that the visit was enthusiastically repeated. Younger sons brought letters from their parents, sending kind love to dear Lady Cowley and regards to his Lordship, with news of illnesses of relations and friends; of poor Mr Canning's death at the Devonshires' villa at Chiswick whither he had gone to recuperate but died in a few days, just as poor Mr Fox had done more than twenty years ago, surely the strangest of coincidences; gossip about engagements and the changing face of Society—all leading up to a recommendation of the bearer, with an eye on his diplomatic preferment, since it was known that Lord Cowley's next posting would be to Paris.

It is perpetually lamented that Society is changing, but this has always been the case. In the hundred years since the first Hanoverian became King of England the balance of power had shifted from the Bedfords, Portlands and Albemarles, to the Devonshires, Hollands (Fox) and Grenvilles, thence to Melbournes, Broughams, Londonderrys. The Hanoverians, even George IV, the most nearly English of them, sat awkwardly on the throne, never at ease with the Whigs who had put them there, preferring the Tory Lords who accepted the Royal prerogative. The House of Hanover had one thing in common with the House of Orange that preceded it, it had come from a rigidly defined society and a manageably small kingdom. Britain's real rulers were its aristocratic landowners who were growing richer all the time; by inter-marriage, by shrewdly compounding with commerce and by acquiring town property— while building tremendous houses to Palladio's designs, any of which outshone the homely royal palaces.

[5] She was the daughter of Baroness de Ros and Lord Henry Fitzgerald, 3rd son of the Duke of Leinst.
[6] He was created Earl Cowley and was also ambassador in Paris.

In 1819 two such families in England had been united, a Grosvenor had married a Leveson-Gower.[7] It was an alliance as much as a marriage, though it was that too. The new American envoy to the Court of St James, wishing to acquaint himself with the ramifications of English Society, asked the Chancellor to name him the two richest Englishmen (who he, honest man, naturally assumed would be nearest to the Throne, and wield influence politically). The reply was cautious; beyond question the Marquess of Stafford and Earl Grosvenor were the richest, but to be influential politically it was not necessary to be more than moderately well-off. No, they and their families were not often seen at Court. If the enquiring American persisted, he would be told that both families had acquired through marriage a vast amount of property; the Staffords owned much of the West Country, and through marriage the north of Scotland; the Grosvenors, as well as owning most of Cheshire and Dorset and part of Wales, were London landlords. Such possessions were in themselves a lifetime's preoccupation, and the peers in question, not ambitious for political preferment, had a high sense of their inherited obligations. At a conservative estimate they lived lives of personal frugality on an annual net income of £200,000. It was as difficult for an American to grasp as that you could spell your name Leveson-Gower and pronounce it Looson-Gaw.

Though much of the Ebury correspondence has been lost, there does exist a batch of letters from Amelie, Countess Cowper[8] to my great grandfather, Robert Grosvenor, whose elder brother, Lord Belgrave, had married Lady Elizabeth Leveson-Gower. They are only interesting because, though she was a vain woman and political intriguer, she was not stupid. She was Palmerston's mistress and eventually married him, had had many lovers and was half ready to fall in love with handsome Bob Grosvenor. He was the recipient of oddly shrewd letters from her all about Canning's craftiness and Wellington's political blunders. 'What a pity! that the Duke was not in love with *me* instead of Mrs. A. . . .'[9] The Moral of the Story is that no Man should ever be in

[7] Daughter of the Marquess of Stafford who was created Duke of Sutherland in 1833, she married Viscount Belgrave, eldest son of the 2nd Earl Grosvenor, created Marquis Westminster in 1831.

[8] Later to be the wife of Lord Palmerston.

[9] Mrs Arbuthnot.

love with a foolish Woman, let him be ever so clever himself, for she will be the ruin of him.'

Bob Grosvenor was not inclined to be in love with *her*, though he had had a slight fancy for her daughter Minny.[10] He desired to *se ranger* himself, having sown his wild oats in the tradition of his class. At some point, probably in 1829, he visited the Cowleys in Vienna and met Charlotte, and instantly decided that he must marry her. Though he was a second son he was a dazzling match for a girl with slightly smirched antecedents for which even having an uncle (Wellington) who was Prime Minister did not compensate. Remembering Society's attitude to the goings-on of the Devonshire House set, one is surprised that Lady Anglesey's lapse from respectability still drew such censure after twenty years. I believe that the reason why the *affaire Paget* was never alluded to in the Grosvenor family (my own mother was not to find out the truth of it until quite late in life), was that Charlotte never lost her painful sensitivity about it. No one would have dreamed of mentioning it in front of a young girl, but servants whispered and older women no doubt scrutinised her through their lorgnettes. Her mother had had lovers other than Henry Paget. Just *whose* daughter might she not be? There was a hard core in England of people like the Staffords, the Salisburys and the Grosvenors who were absolutely intolerant of loose behaviour, but their great wealth, unassailable position, and strict principles, made them respected; beside them the crude permissiveness of Carlton House and the Pavilion at Brighton dimmed like tinsel in daylight.

To the Cowleys Robert Grosvenor must have seemed like an answer to prayer. I try to put out of my mind the picture of my great-grandfather as the vain old man remembered by my mother and older cousins, and see him as he must have looked to Charlotte, tall and slight with the long curling Grosvenor mouth that even in repose seemed to be smiling.

Younger sons were expected to take on the family constituencies so Robert stood first for Shaftesbury, owned by his mother's family, the Egertons, and then for Chester, and rode fairly lightly to Parliamentary demands. One feels that the House of Commons was to him just another club to join, less amusing than Brooks'. In later life as Lord Ebury he became assiduous about attending the

[10] Who became the wife of Lord Shaftesbury.

House of Lords, an elderly Tory peer fumbling with his pince-nez in order to read long memoranda on Church politics which emptied the Chamber. He was a handsome old man as he had been a handsome young one, and to foreigners a perfect example of *'le vieux milord Anglais'*.

'Reveller Bob', as his sister-in-law, Elizabeth Belgrave, nicknamed him when they were both young, went with Sir Alexander Malet, who was attaché to the British Embassy in Russia, in 1825, to represent, in a general and unspecified way, the *jeunesse dorée* of Britain on the occasion of the crowning of the new Czar. The two young men enjoyed themselves hugely and the parties given at the British Embassy easily outshone those given by Marmont, the French Ambassador. After the coronation the two friends escaped to go bear shooting in southern Russia. Sir Alexander in his letters speaks with warmth of the easy good temper of his companion which no cold or discomfort ever ruffled. In fact nothing in his life ever ruffled Robert. Lady Cowper was not the only married woman to try to attract him, Lady Blessington asked him to her most *intime* parties, D'Orsay cultivated him. He was the fashion and in his smiling easy way accepted the situation as his due.

Young Lady Harrowby writing to her mother Lady Bute in 1827 describes the *haute monde* with a schoolgirl's relish, and one particular party with infectious glee. Boyle Farm out at Chiswick belonged to Lord Henry Fitzgerald, who lent it for a mid-summer fête that June to five young men, Lord Chesterfield, Lord Castlereagh, Lord Alvanley, Henry de Ros, and Bob Grosvenor. Susan Harrowby's pleasure at all she sees runs out of adjectives:

'I never saw such a pretty fête as it was—nothing was spared to embellish it in every possible way. You may imagine those five young men all laying their heads together! It succeeded to perfection. Such a fine day, such a pretty place, such heaps of pretty faces. Nothing in the least degree *manqué* and all the *flower* of England there . . . one of the five stepped forward and presented a bouquet to every lady as she arrived, so everybody had flowers in their hands and the gentlemen mostly had roses in their coats. There were a great many young ladies (of) about 25, all the *choicest*, who were dressed alike and called themselves *Rosières*, having a wreath of white roses going across their skirts from the sash to the trimming (flounce). These danced in quadrilles with no other ladies. . . .'

From boats on the river, leading singers from the Opera sang. 'Besides all this dancing and singing there were the prettiest possible illuminations—a sort of Vauxhall thing, but so very tastefully done. Fireworks were arranged on a little island in the River and the reflections in the water were so very beautiful, one saw boats gliding about looking all dark against the light . . . then there were numbers of common people ranged on the opposite shore, enjoying the Fête so, they had probably never seen fireworks and their hurrahing was delightful I thought.'

A creamy syllabub of entertainment, whipped up on the spur of the moment, in which patrician young men in the becoming close-fitting clothes of the day, and fresh girls with their hands full of roses, added piquancy to the scene, while at a distance a hurrahing populace watched fireworks flowering up into the night sky. It seems to give credence to today's popular novelistic view of the Regency period, making a romantic *genre* painting of an age (and a class) that was fully as sordid and striving as any other before or since. Of the hosts one (Alvanley) was a vicious brute and one (de Ros) a drunkard.

Bob Grosvenor and his brother Belgrave's wife had been friends from their first meeting. 'We all scream and laugh at his jokes, he is full of entertainment and fun and is a most amiable creature and easy friend,' she wrote of him. Elizabeth Belgrave, no fool, saw that this *farceur* needed a wife who would balance his natural ebullience with dignity and good sense. 'Not in the least bit giddy,' she said after meeting Charlotte Wellesley, 'or thinking of her own amusement, but sensible and acting for herself with a great deal of thought and a sort of dignity which is particularly right in her position.'

She wrote to Robert: 'I take her to be a person of a great deal of feeling and susceptibility, and so much aware of the difficulties of her situation as to be quite painfully anxious as to whether she will be well-liked.' (This could have been a gentle hint that the prospective bridegroom must mend his easy ways with ladies.) To her mother, Elizabeth wrote of Charlotte: 'Having had so much of the *désagréments* of life, she will the better appreciate being well treated. From all I hear I should think her the very reverse of Robert, grave and thoughtful, which will be all the better.' Easy enough to say, but life is not to be calmly parcelled off or human beings placed in pigeon-holes. Charlotte's wounded and sensitive heart, concealed under a composed exterior, needed much more subtle handling than Reveller Bob was able to give her. She laughed seldom and rarely smiled at his absurdities. It was part of her charm for him.

At Eaton she made an excellent impression on Robert's parents. She was reserved but she was not timid. She was a daring rider to hounds and could whip a four-in-hand through the traffic in Piccadilly to the admiration of the Grosvenor's old coachman. A granddaughter who only remembered her when bent and old, told me that one felt an imperious will kept under iron control, remembered too that she had eyes of star-sapphire blue, and a mouth at once generous and firm with lips that even in old age were truly cherry red.

They were married, Robert Victor and Charlotte Arbuthnot, at St George's Church, Hanover Square, the Duke of Wellington giving the bride away, in the beautiful May weather of the year 1831. Posed wedding groups are nearly always stiff. The painting by Charles Leslie RA of the Grosvenor family gathered together in the Picture Gallery of Grosvenor House soon after the wedding is no exception. Only two little Belgrave children who have let a parrot out of its cage provide relief, and even they look solemn.

In 1805 Lord Grosvenor, Robert's father, had, on the death of George III's brother, acquired the Crown lease of Gloucester House, the garden of which bordered a lane that divided it from Hyde Park. It was not an impressive house, it was in fact rather plain and countryfied with a shallow forecourt onto what was to be Upper Grosvenor Street. The rooms were small and ill-lit.

By now Lord Grosvenor had become established as a collector of paintings of the first rank (which accounts for Wellington sending his dear Lord Robert a request to act for him in the purchase of a landscape by Adam Pinaker, a commission which Robert was happy to carry out for his wife's uncle though being himself without the least interest in pictures except as wall coverings). Such paintings as the late royal duke possessed had been removed to Windsor; Porden, who had remodelled Eaton, was commanded to design a new picture gallery that would have an impressive façade on the garden front. By the time Robert and Charlotte were married this had been completed; later Cundy was to design a new screen with Doric columns on the street side.

Collector's mania was in the air, Lord Grosvenor vying with his son Belgrave's father-in-law Lord Stafford, in his acquisition of masterpieces which included the Rubens 'Adoration of the Magi', and four other canvases of his, looted by Marshal Soult from a convent near Madrid, the finest of which, 'Abraham receiving bread from Melchisedek' fills in the background of Leslie's family group. Velasquez's 'Don Balthasar Carlos on his pony' hangs above the pianoforte on which the new Marchioness is playing for the children to dance.[11] Robert, who on his marriage to Wellington's niece had been made Comptroller of the Royal Household to William IV, is leaning against a cabinet in court dress, in a relaxed attitude which emphasises the length of his elegant legs, he and Charlotte having just come from a Drawing Room; she is stiffly upheld by her wedding dress of white satin with leg-o-mutton sleeves, her little face haloed by a huge satin bonnet with orange blossom under the brim, and stands nervously clasping her parasol, the sky-light in the high coved ceiling pouring light down on her— not yet relaxed, not quite one of the family. The painting demonstrates family solidarity and *bienséance*, and apart from the pictures and furnishings, money carefully spent without ostentation, all the ladies but the bride are extremely plainly dressed.

The Robert Grosvenors spent the first fourteen years of their married life in No. 35 Park Street, off Upper Grosvenor Street, which Lord Grosvenor put at their disposal. Like No. 30, in which my grandmother, Charlotte's daughter-in-law lived, No. 35 was part of the Grosvenor House complex, a tall baldish house of stuccoed brick with a number of blank windows on the street side. It conveyed nothing to me as a young girl to be told that it was where my Ebury great-grandparents had lived. Not till much later did I begin to visualise them as real people, who could conceivably once have been as young as I was. The destruction of one side of the street and of Grosvenor House itself for the purpose of building a mammoth hotel, to be named after it, was just one more thing to make one's elders sigh. I had always seen, but had not particularly noticed, that No. 35 Park Street (then still standing) had a looking-glass fixed at an angle to the porch of the front door. Charlotte's sitting-room was on the ground floor, looking up the street; she was thus able to glance quickly between the curtains

[11] That year Earl Grosvenor had received a Marquisate.

when the doorbell rang and see in the mirror who her callers were.
If a black barouche bearing the Paget crest drawn by four black
horses with postilions containing her mother, Lady Anglesey, drew
up at her door she was able to warn the footman that she was at
home *to no one else*. If Lady Cowley, her stepmother, happened to
be already with her, the Anglesey carriage would be turned away.

*The Robert Grosvenors and Albertine:
done on the pier at Brighton*

4

Married Life among the Grosvenors

The year Lord Grosvenor, Charlotte's father-in-law, was created Marquis Westminster, in 1831, the Belgraves became 'the young Grosvenors', and long visits to Eaton were obligatory, boring Charlotte as well they might, but having to be endured since Robert was such a favourite there, his parents adoring him, his elder brother finding him an indispensable ally. The Reform Bill had received the Royal assent and constituencies were being reformed; Robert's own seat, Chester City, was retained and he was returned there after the General Election that followed the passing of the Bill.

At this distance it is difficult to detach these people from their backgrounds. The Wortleys do not present any difficulty because in their letters they were perfectly simple and open, could laugh at themselves and all dearly loved Wortley. It is hard to imagine that anyone could have loved Eaton as remodelled by William Porden (though it was in outline at least, sober in comparison with what was to follow).

The first Eaton had been built by Samwell in the time of Charles II. Porden replaced it with a piece of monumental but not 'mongrel' Gothic as Greville, writing later in the Victorian century, described its successor: 'a monument to wealth, ignorance and bad taste.' This was after the architect Waterhouse had been allowed in the '70s to remodel Porden's Eaton on the scale of his Natural History Museum in South Kensington (the two stood for examples of the ultimate horrors of Victorian architecture and gave the era in building known as 'Victorian' a bad name).

Porden's Eaton was cold and comfortless and grandly Gothic, covering many acres of ground, its saloons had corresponding acres of carpet in an impressive Gothic design; being so large the rooms were never light, perpetual dusk hanging about the heavy cornices. There were still rooms of this size in country houses when the writer was a young girl and the temptation was to whisper and tiptoe in them as if one was in church. Hostesses tried to make little oases under the lamps with signed photographs in silver frames, and a small scatter of personal possessions, but to very little effect. The hostess had a room of her own, of course, that had gilt flower baskets kept filled up by the head-gardener with a succession of gloxinias, calceolarias and schiazanthus. It would have unglazed bookcases full of poetry and devotional books, an embroidery frame, an inadequate fire in a small steel basket-grate and, as in Lady Marchmain's boudoir at Brideshead, a good deal of *'bondieuserie'*. At Moor Park the sons' wives, rather than brave the draughts downstairs, huddled in each other's firelit bedrooms, which had broad window seats overlooking the pleasure grounds.

Her Wellesley relations need not have feared for Charlotte, she was not going to be a bolter, but she was to grow every year more serious-minded, more bent on self-improvement. She schooled herself in patience and forbearance, since the defects of her character were that she was by nature intolerant and, in human relationships, wary. She tried hard to balance Robert's natural levity with seriousness. On one occasion, when her appearance on the grand staircase at Eaton dressed in white drew appreciative exclamations from the assembled guests below, she turned and went back to her room and got her maid to put her into her plainest oldest dress; an example of the Wellesley contrariness, and there must have been many more.

Not that the Grosvenors were not themselves high-minded. They were always conscious that they were guardians of great and largely untapped wealth; their sense of duty toward this inheritance amounted to an obsession. They *had* to excel, being who they were; everything they did had to be done better than anyone else could do it, down to their amusements—racing, shooting and fishing—for which pursuits they owned the finest facilities in the kingdom.

Elizabeth Belgrave thought Charlotte's delicate sense of her equivocal situation as the daughter of an adulteress most admirable, and, kind woman that she was, tried to draw her into the sort of drawing-room theatricals fashionable at this time by which the dullness of evenings at Eaton were alleviated. Lady Cowper thought that Bob should have been an actor, so well did he take his part in these. A glimpse of the older Grosvenors at home comes from an unexpected source: a Journal kept by Sophia Mytton, daughter of the Rector of Eccleston, who had one of the

family livings. (The Belgraves had by now been married for three
years, Robert was as yet unmarried.)

Sophia writes:

'*January 1st. 1822.* We went to Chester School in the morning to
see the prizes given. Dined at Eaton, a party of twenty three. I sat
at dinner between Lord Grosvenor and Mr. Gleney (the curate).
Lord G. all fun and good humour, making us drink champagne,
and asking us if we had ever been tipsy; at dessert Ld. Wilton,
Mr. Ayckbourne (the agent) and Mr. Gleney, sang three very
pretty glees; as soon as we retired to the Drawing room, Dumb
Crambo was proposed. Ld. Wilton was then very urgent for Hen
and Chickens, but out of compassion for our clothes, it was given
up and Blind Man's Bluff fixed upon, which was excellent fun. To
complete this delightful evening, the Pianoforte was brought out
of the Saloon and we danced Quadrilles. I danced with Ld. and
Mr. Stanley, both pleasant and very good natured. Lady Wilton
looked quite beautiful and her husband no less so, who cd produce
such a pair for perfect elegance? The only thing wanting was the
Reveller Bob, as Lady Wilton called him, who was otherwise
employed, having that very day begun with the Scarlatina.

'*Jany 23rd.* Ld. Belgrave came here for two days hunting. Papa
wrote to Eaton to invite them all, or any of them, to dine here on
Thursday, as Ld. B. was not allowed to go near the house for fear
of infection. The following note arrived at eleven o'clock at night
in answer to the invitation—

> "My father won't eat
> My mother is infectious,
> Wilton is same, and asleep,
> Lady Wilton has spoiled her best gown,
> And yours most truly Robert Grosvenor is not invited."

'*Feb. 1st.* We dined at Eaton, the Belgraves, Wiltons, Robert
Grosvenor, Mr. A. and Mr. Webb (another curate) were the party.
Ld. Grosvenor and Ld Wilton were my neighbours at dinner;
Harriet (her sister) sat by Robert but he seemed low, for he did
not chatter and roar as he generally does. I overheard part of a
conversation concerning the Creation, between Ld. Belgrave, Lady
Grosvenor and Mr. Ayckbourne; the two latter agreed with her
opinion that the world was chaos previous to the Creation, and
made out of nothing; Ld. B. then said that it had often occurred to

him that it might be otherwise, for it is written "He gathered together the waters", which plainly showed that it was not void entirely before the Creation. I lost a great deal then to my sorrow, and when next I had an opportunity of listening Lady G. seemed *un peu opiniatre*, and cd not, wd not, understand Lord B. but said that his opinion was contrary to some parts of the Bible. Mr. A. assured her that Ld. Belgrave did not mean to invalidate the Scriptures, upon which there was such a laughing that the rest of his speech went to the winds, and he was silent, but Lady G. and Ld B. continued their dispute till prayer time—after prayers we took our leave and Ld. Wilton handed us into the Coach, and there ended our short but pleasant visit.'

Benevolence toward the Rectory girls was all very laudable, but ten years later at Eaton they were still shrieking over Dumb Crambo to Charlotte's infinite boredom. The affection between the Wiltons had cooled. Elizabeth Belgrave writing in 1831, the year of Robert's marriage, said that the Wiltons took no pains to make themselves agreeable and embarrassed everyone by quarrelling in public. She was all the more delighted with Robert's quiet Charlotte whose dread of 'scenes' was such that she would leave the room if one was remotely threatened.

As part of a large united affectionate family it was fatally easy to be sucked into the family orbit and move mindlessly round from race meeting to race meeting, to Highland Gatherings, Church Bazaars and Charity Balls. There is a pen and ink drawing of Charlotte at a Chester Bazaar by Elizabeth Belgrave who had a clever knack with likenesses. She is standing on a footstool ('worked by Lady R. Grosvenor, every stitch counted and the raw materials alone worth £3 17s 8½d') in the character of a Herald with a pin-cushion on her head in the shape of a candle extinguisher ('not to be procured at any other bazaar').

My heart goes out to Charlotte, newly married, perched on that wretched footstool, anxiously trying to look as if she is enjoying herself. It is fair to say that she would not have envisaged any other kind of life for herself, nor imagined any other environment. (Years and years later when she was growing old, trapped like a little black fly in a monumental piece of amber, her favourite son and his wife and daughters with full family approval, left Moor Park to live in a small house in London; there to have freedom to paint and compose and entertain artists and musicians, while in no way contravening the conventions of their class. No one thought of labelling the Norman Grosvenors *déclassés*, as would have been the case forty years earlier.)

Trapped Charlotte was, but not without spirit to observe and comment. In one of the tin boxes I have mentioned I find a clue to her in an undated pen and ink drawing on a piece of gilt-edged paper initialled C.A.W. It was the fashion to produce a *jeu d'esprit* for an album such as all young girls possessed—it whiled away the time while the men were playing billiards or sleeping off the day's sport in the smoking room.

The drawing is of an imaginary terrain called *The Regions of Bore*. The way to this country is by '*the slippery road of Admiration*'. The country is bounded by unscaleable brass walls, which have four entrances (no exits). Over one of the entrances are the terrible words '*Lasciate ogni speranza voi chi entrate*',[1] seen by Dante written up over the mouth of Hell. The other three presumably represent St James's, Piccadilly, St Mary's, Chester, and St George's, Hanover Square. The traveller will be lucky if he does not fall into the marshes of *Obstinacy* and *Bad Advice* which border the road of *Admiration* leading to the entrance. Once inside, the region becomes perilous, it is threatened by a river called *Misery*, between woods called *Bore* and rocks called '*Money Matters*', '*Contradiction*', '*Disgust*', and '*Jealousy*', round a '*Bottomless Pit of Despondency*'. Most revealing are the words scribbled under the drawing: 'There are certain *ignis fatuis* that frequent these marshes, rank, riches, diamonds, carriages, etc. etc.'

A smouldering here of something resented, perhaps the endless talk about marrying money such as only the very rich indulge in. Charlotte had a horror of ostentation and was once to say of a harmless guest, 'nasty vulgar woman, wear diamonds in the daytime—' (only in the language of her class she would have said 'dimonds' and 'nesty').

In 1922 when Moor Park was sold to Leverhulme, Charlotte's letters disappeared with the rest of the family papers. So few came into my hands that I cannot follow the workings of her mind through the years as I can those of Caroline Wharncliffe from her letters. I must understand her from what slight evidence there is, while feeling that the ice I am treading is very thin. Disraeli wrote

---

[1] 'Abandon hope all ye who enter here'.

of Charlotte: 'Lady Ebury said she lived for climate and the affections, two good things', but this is not much to build a character on.

I piece together the fragments, finding her in January 1833 at Hatfield at a delightful party (very unlike those games at Eaton of Hen and Chickens). The Salisburys held an entertainment yearly in which they all took part and their friends as well. Frances Cecil and Charlotte Wellesley had become friends in Vienna when the Salisburys went out there to stay with the Cowleys (Lady Cowley it will be remembered was Lord Salisbury's aunt and Charlotte's step-mother). This year it was to be Tableaux Vivants; the subject, *The Waverley Novels*. In the hall of Hatfield with its chessboard floor of black and white marble, the rank and beauty of England were grouped. In the Talisman tableau Lady Salisbury, tall and pale, was Edith Plantagenet, Lady Robert Grosvenor, her reddish fair hair in long plaits, was an appealing Berengaria, Lord Hillsborough the perfect Coeur de Lion. One would like to know what part Reveller Bob was given, Saladin perhaps. He excelled at drawing-room theatricals.

Charlotte's fondness for Frances Salisbury for some reason not now discoverable, cooled.

In her diary for November 4th, 1836, Frances records, 'I had a very painful interview with Lady R. Grosvenor. She reproached me with all my conduct to her since her marriage—I think without foundation. Sure I am that I have been the sufferer and that she deserted me before my sentiments suffered any change. She made me miserable by her altered conduct—but that is over, and feelings that have once been destroyed cannot be revived. She parted from me in anger, and I conclude we are parted for ever . . .'

Thursday December 8th, 1836. 'I told the Duke (Wellington) all that had passed between me and Lady Robert. He said that hers was the same turn of mind that existed in others of her family, particularly Lord Cowley and his brother Gerald[2]—an unfortunate disposition to suspect her best friends and think herself neglected by them. And speaking with much feeling he said, "One can only pity those who are subject to such unfortunate feelings, and do all one can to show them how groundless they are. Have you written

---

[2] The Dean of Durham. His divorce from Emily Cadogan had spoilt his chance of getting a bishopric, and this he blamed on his brothers, who had all achieved fame with apparent ease.

to her since?" I said "No". He looked surprised—"What, have
you done nothing? Write to her by all means, immediately, the
kindest letter you can". I did.'

Three years later Frances was dead, and Lord Salisbury was
sending Charlotte a bracelet of 'her once dear Fanny's'. Just what
had it all been about?

After Victoria, Robert, Norman, Algy and Dick, Charlotte might
have been excused for thinking that by adding Albertine as a
companion for Victoria (who had got a twelve year start) she had
done her duty by the Grosvenors. Her Uncle Arthur had reminded
her, when the love-affair in Vienna had set the Wellesleys raking
over the ashes of the Anglesey scandal, that she had a duty to her
name. Well, she had obeyed him, married with his approval, called
a boy (who died) after him. By the time her children were all born,
by 1844 when she was thirty-seven, she was externally still the
same composed creature of the Leslie family group, making the
least of herself in dull dresses and dowdy caps.

By this time the Anglesey-Wellesley scandal seems to have been
decently interred. At all events the children of the Chelsea con-
nection came to stay at Moor Park, the Ladies Augusta and Honoria
Cadogan, daughters of Char's uncle, Lord Chelsea; their spirited
water-colour drawings of family life *chez* the Eburys briefly lift
the curtain for us.

The parents, at some personal sacrifice, would remove the
children to the sea whenever the servants had to have holidays.
There are charming silhouettes done on the pier at Brighton
(Brighton air was sovereign for every ill, for Albertine's throats
and her father's weak chest). Robert has long curling hair and
Char an incipient Wellesley nose. There is a water-colour sketch of
an Alpine expedition with all the ladies bedded down in a barn on
a row of camp beds, bonnets and dresses hanging from nails, with
a screen to conceal the *necessaire*, and Lady R.G. and 'Dabbins'
(Norman) the baby, hidden behind an arrangement of rugs held
up with clothes pegs.

A privileged grandchild (my mother), playing indoors on a
rainy day beside an enormous high bed in which her grandmother
(Charlotte) lies apparently suspended between Heaven and Earth,
asks to be told all over again the story of the prints, the pencil
sketches and the glassy brown photographs that cover every inch

of the walls. The amused deep voice supplies the answer: 'That was your grandfather when we were first married, he had just come from the King,' (what King?), 'and that is your aunt Victoria on the beach at Walmer when she was younger than you,' (but are aunts ever young?), 'and that one,' (the old bent man with the nose like Mr Punch?), 'that was my Uncle Arthur who saved England. The man who beat Boney.'

From Lady Salisbury's Journal we get a glimpse of the old Duke's great fondness for the small fry among his relations; with his invariable kindness he asked the Robert Grosvenor children to stay while Charlotte took Robert, whose chest had never been strong, abroad after a bout of pneumonia. The Duke had not himself been happily married and admitted it; he frightened his wife into lying to him. He perceived that his niece was not entirely happy. The only concern he could show her was the practical help of having her children to stay at Walmer Castle, his by right of his being Warden of the Cinque Ports. The R.G.'s children treated him as if he were their own age. Bo (Robert) was greedy as was Oggy (Victoria), and they were not, it seems, restrained from overeating. 'We are now eight children in this house,' wrote Lady Salisbury on one of these occasions from Stratfield Saye, 'three of mine, three de Ros, two Grosvenors—and the rush of delight when the Duke enters the room and the way in which they surround his chair is quite *touchant*.' (Pleasant to picture those shining ringlets, bunchy petticoats and nankeen trousers, submerging their playmate, the old Punchinello, in his deep armchair.)

Oggy and Bo remembered the Duke on the beach at Walmer, striding about in his inflatable topcoat, pooh-poohing the nurse's fears about the sea being too cold for the children to bathe—the Album has another vivid pen and ink sketch probably by Olivia Cowley (who, it will be remembered, married young Henry Wellesley) of her children in a high wind by a tumultuous sea, upon which a steam packet is tossing, the baby being nearly blown out of the nurse's arms, she, poor woman, exclaiming piteously, 'Must we cross, your Grace?' to which he is replying by sternly pointing to the pitching vessel.

My grandmother Caroline's eldest sister Mary was a small child in 1852, the year in which Wellington died, at an age when impressions bite deep. Her parents rented a house in Carlton Gardens

overlooking the Mall. 'When I search these early memories,' she
wrote for me, 'there comes one so far back and dreamlike, that I
wonder if it can really have happened. I was a very small girl and
someone woke me in the middle of the night and carried me to the
nursery window. And there, slowly passing along the Mall in the
darkness was a great lumbering Thing on which flickering lights
showed here and there on broad gleams of scarlet and gold. And
there was the trampling of many horses, and jingle of bits and
spurs, and then gradually the lights faded and the sounds died
away, and they said to me, "Now you must always remember that
you have seen the great Duke of Wellington's funeral." ' This was
puzzling, and when she was older she concluded that, 'It could not
have been exactly that, for the Duke was carried to his grave (in
St Paul's) by broad daylight and through a great concourse of
people. I think it must have been the passing of the coffin on its
way from Stratfield Saye to Chelsea Hospital, there to lie in state
for some hours or days . . .'

The loss to England of such a man was so tremendous that
private grief seemed out of place; among her family in the choir-
stalls of St Paul's Charlotte wept quietly, not for the man who beat
Boney but for the uncle who had cared for her. 'As the *cortège*
entered the Cathedral the hat on the coffin seemed for a moment
to wake into life, a wind whispered in the aisles of the great
church, the plumes fluttered, shivered, and were still.'[3]

At the end of the eighteenth century the estate of Moor Park in
Hertfordshire, then deep country, now on the Greater London
District Line, had come into the market on the death of a Mr
Robert Williams, a banker. He had bought it from an East India
merchant, a Mr Rous, who in turn had bought it from Sir Lawrence
Dundas, a man of great taste which neither Mr Rous nor Mr
Williams was. They were businessmen who fancied bettering their
station in life.

Where the present-day Moor Park stands was once a matchless
Jacobean house,[4] the house which Sir William Temple called
'—the sweetest place, I think, that I have seen in my life, either

---

[3] *The Sword of State* by Susan Buchan (Lady Tweedsmuir).
[4] Robert Grosvenor when he came to live at Moor Park in the eighteen-
forties pulled down two small and perfect Jacobean lodges in the park,
saying that his relations would always want to be borrowing them!

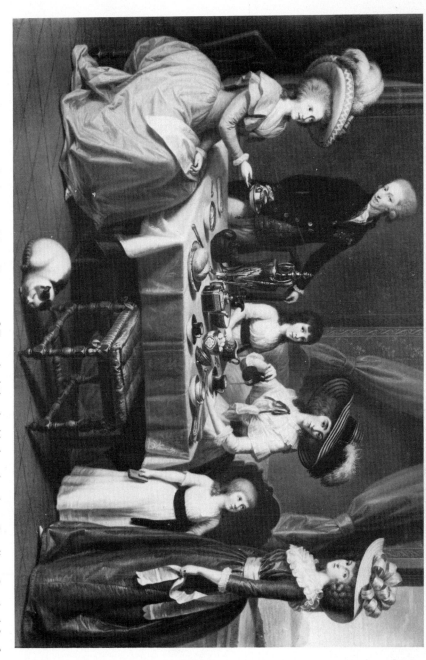

The Evian breakfast party. The hostess, Mary Countess of Erne, is sitting beside her daughter Caroline. On the left of the picture are the Prince and Princess of Piedmont, on the right Lady Hervey and her daughter Eliza. In the foreground

Wharncliffe House in Curzon Street, now known as Crewe House and the property of Thomas Tilling Ltd.

Moor Park, Hertfordshire; the seat of Sir Lawrence Dundas, by Richard Wilson. Reproduced by permission of the Marquis of Zetland and the Courtauld Institute of Art.

insisted – A.C. yielded –
marble Halls not in her line – (Cows tail considered successful

Pencil drawing by Lady Augusta Cadogan of a corner of the hall at
Moor Park.

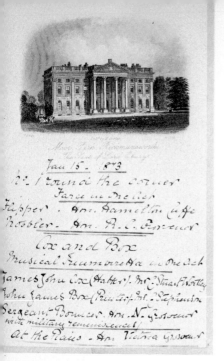

Theatricals at Moor Park; the first performance on any stage of W.S. Gilbert's 'Box and Cox'.

Charlotte in the character of a herald at the Chester Bazaar.

Two Grosvenor children drawn by their aunt, Olivia de Ros, Countess Cowley.

Victoria with her donkeys.

The hall of No. 30 Upper Grosvenor Street, now demolished.

The Robert Grosvenors riding in the Row with Albertine.

Norman and Caroline at the time of their engagement.

Norman resting, by Sir W.S. Gilbert.

The girls of James's. Left to right: Blanche, Mrs Frederick Firebrace; Caroline, the Hon Mrs Norman Grosvenor; Margaret, the Hon Lady Talbot; Katharine, the Hon Lady Lyttleton; and with her back turned, Mary, Countess of Lovelace, the artist.

The Hon Jane Lawley, daughter of the first Lord Wenlock, by Sir Francis
Grant PRA, reproduced by permission of Mr R.A. Cecil.

Susan Grosvenor, at the time of her marriage to John Buchan.

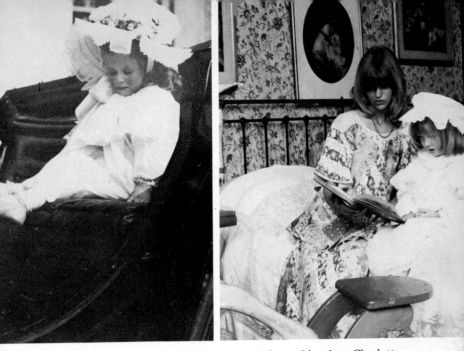

The author, aged four; her daughter Emma and granddaughter Charlotte, aged four.

On a family holiday. John Buchan, his three sons, Alistair, William and John, his daughter Alice and son-in-law Brian Fairfax-Lucy, with Buster.

The author at Charlecote, by John Morley. By permission of the artist.

before or since, at home or abroad.' He spent his honeymoon with
Dorothy Osborne there in 1655. The house which was later the
Duke of Monmouth's, had a garden made in the first quarter of
the seventeenth century by Lucy, Countess of Bedford, acknow-
ledged the finest in England for its profusion of rare plants, its
water-pieces, its walks of shade. It belonged to an age when people
thought it right to indulge a mood of civilised melancholy by
stretching out on a grassy bank with a volume of verse within
hearing of a fountain's plashing. Temple's was the taste of his
period. He loved the formality of auricules with their purple-
rimmed eyes and tulips fantastically feathered and striped, writing:
'Whoever observes the work upon the best Indian gowns, or the
painting on their best screens and porcelains, will find their beauty
is all of this kind.'

Horace Walpole thought differently. His comment on the Moor
Park garden was: 'any man might design and build as sweet a
garden who had been born in and never stirred out of Holborn.'
He was no better pleased with the landscaping wrought by
Capability Brown for its next owner: 'I was not much struck with
it, after all the miracles I had heard Brown had performed there.
He has undulated the horizon in so many artificial mole-hills that
it is full as unnatural as if it were drawn with a rule and compass.'
Temple, remembering it, later wrote: '—of what it is now I can
give little account, (it) having passed through several hands that
have made great changes in the gardens as well as (the) house; but
the remembrance of what it was is too pleasant ever to forget,
therefore I do not believe to have mistaken the figure of it, which
may serve as a pattern for the best gardens of our manner . . .'

The garden he remembered was a descendant of the Elizabethan
gardens that were the settings of Shakespeare's pastoral comedies,
walled by trim hedges against the wind, cushioned underfoot by
herbs, sending up bruised scents of thyme and musk and camomile.
It was inevitable—once the place passed from Monmouth's widow
(he had lived there after the discovery of the Ryehouse Plot and
his banishment from Court)—into the possession of a rich businessman, that all about it, house, garden, policies, should suffer change
in line with the taste of the day.

Its new owner, Benjamin Styles, had been one of the promoters
of the South Sea Company of which his brother-in-law was a
governor. He bought Moor Park in 1720, encased the Jacobean

C

house in a shell of white Portland stone and gave it a four-columned portico of which the Corinthian capitals alone were six feet high, under a grand pediment. Magnificence was all. The central block was connected to a chapel and kitchens by a curving colonnade of great elegance.

Styles was a rich man and an astute one (forewarned, he got out of the South Sea Company before the bubble burst), and he called in the best craftsmen of the time. Sir James Thornhill was his choice for the architect of the house and its interior decoration, and in the main it is his house that stands today. Owing to changes of ownership since Styles almost all documents relating to the building of it have vanished. What we do know is that Thornhill displeased Styles by overcharging for the eight allegorical paintings which were to decorate the Central Hall which rises to the whole height of the building, and the Great Circle in the Ceiling (in the manner of St Peter's in Rome) to give it the appearance of a dome. Styles expected a lot for his money. The paintings, he said, were poorly executed and would fade and deaden with time. Thornhill wrote to him that 'a little Picture Varnish laid on by the most Ordinary hand at small Expense would refresh and recover them' but refused, himself, to undertake this unless paid more. He had bought South Sea stock on Styles' advice and been obliged to sell some of it to pay his workmen, the work, as invariably happens, having outrun the estimate. He had a justified grievance. The lawsuit that followed was decided in his favour.

By the time that Moor Park passed to Lord Anson, the victor of Finisterre, it was a considerable palace. Thornhill's paintings for the Hall having presumably 'deadened', they had been replaced by eight others by Amiconi, of the loves of Jupiter and Io, though the Dome and some allegorical paintings by Thornhill survive in the Saloon, dark and unimpressive. On the staircase Sleter painted the Rape of Proserpine and figures in grisaille round the Gallery. Styles' insistence on magnificence ran into tastelessness with five heavily pedimented door-cases of marble bearing life-sized figures of all the Virtues, repeated round the Gallery above.

From Lord Anson Moor Park passed to Sir Lawrence Dundas, a patron of Richard Wilson. He it was who commissioned Cipriani to decorate the coved ceiling of the long Drawing Room, with its view of descending terraces and Capability's 'artificial mole-hills', with delicate figures set in a frame of finest gilt scroll-work, and to design for it a marble chimney-piece supported by goddesses with a frieze of 'the dancing hours', girls with linked hands fluttering against a background of lapis-lazuli.

Altogether the house was the work of great craftsmen; possibly Leoni, carrying on where Thornhill left off after the law-suit, Baguti, most probably responsible for the door-cases and the plaster-work of military trophies. And to Robert Adam is attributed the gallery with its gilt balustrading, at least one of the fireplaces, the splendid ceilings, and the ornate console tables[5] that by the Grosvenors were piled with old newspapers, tracts, parish magazines, and other homely impedimenta. Rous, the last owner before Lord Grosvenor bought Moor Park, pulled down the graceful colonnading which balanced the central block and made sense of Thornhill's design, found himself short of money, and sold the stones.

Moor Park was a place upon which in two hundred years an enormous amount of money had been spent. Lord Grosvenor, as a great spender himself, respected this fact. Robert and Charlotte would not need to spend anything further (he liked to practise small economies) since much of the furniture bought for the house by Dundas had descended through two successive owners and was still in the rooms.

As Groom of the Stole and Treasurer of the Household Robert had to be in London for the greater part of the year. He was, as well, MP for Chester. So in fact they did not take possession of Moor Park until 1845, the year of Lord Westminster's death and the accession of Robert's brother Belgrave, father of the first Duke. Having been given this handsome house they did not question its suitability.

During the years it became, as far as its heroic proportions allowed, cosy; fittings for oil and gas lamps replaced the Adam torchères, a hideous drugget of red and yellow felt was laid down in the Hall, a billiard table was installed, also a harmonium for evening hymn singing, and racks for billiard cues and croquet mallets stood beneath the Amiconi paintings of the loves of Jupiter. At this point, two grand-daughters of Charlotte's contribute their recollections: Marnie[6] wrote: 'I do not remember very much about the furniture of our nursery, excepting the

[5] Now at Kenwood House.
[6] Mrs Jeremy Peyton-Jones.

chairs—three or four armchairs painted with garlands of flowers on a dark green background and with delicate cane seats. I have since realised that they were particularly exquisite examples of Hepplewhite's art, banished to the nursery by Griekie (our grandmother) who far preferred solid mahogany well upholstered with red plush or tapestry . . .' And Maudie:[7] 'Once when playing in the attics with my brother Hughie I came on a set of furniture which I now know to have been designed for the house by Robert Adam, wrapped in sheets of the *Times* newspaper of 1845 . . .'

This suite, banished to the attics as soon as the Robert Grosvenors took possession, consisted of fauteuils, settees with scrolled ends, armchairs and stools, all with gilt rams' heads and legs tapering to little gilt hooves. It was to have an adventurous history. Sold by Leverhulme to America in 1926 some pieces found their way to the White House. These were brought back to England through the public spirit of a Bond Street dealer who offered them to the nation as examples of an important period of English furniture design, at a sixth of their value. They are now happily at Kenwood.

So my great-grandparents settled in what was to be their married home. Not rapturous as Caroline and James Stuart Wortley had been on first discovering Wortley but not disillusioned or regretful; once a marriage in their circle had been undertaken any inadequacies in it were kept out of sight. By now, 1845, Charlotte's child-bearing years were over. They had taken toll of her slight strength, she disliked small babies only finding them interesting when they could talk and she read aloud to them. Two years after their marriage Caroline Wharncliffe had written to her daughter from the Brighton Pavilion where she and the Doge were staying with King William and Queen Adelaide: 'By the by, Lady R. Grosvenor is going to town either Saturday or Monday and begg'd I would tell you so, and as you were both great walkers she hoped you would call on her, as she would upon you. I like her very much; the menage seems to go on beautifully. They walk together every day and appear most comfortable. She improved much upon acquaintance; but she is not in beauty just now, being too thin and not looking strong' (in a word, pregnant with Bo).

'Comfortable' was Caroline's favourite word, it seems to sum up

[7] The Hon. Mrs Maurice Glyn.

her loving uncritical nature, to her it meant the climate of a companionship in which either could speak what was in his or her mind and be at once intuitively understood. I doubt if being married to Charlotte was comfortable in that sense. Inherited family characteristics and the shadow over her early years had made her too wary of intimacy. But Wharncliffe House in Curzon Street, the London house of Caroline's parents, and 35 Park Street were not far apart and these two great walkers, one imagines, commenced a friendship then that was to be carried on into another generation and to end in intermarriage between the families of Wortley and Grosvenor.

The Robert Grosvenors lived very much at the centre of their world. Melbourne had offered Robert on his marriage the post of Comptroller of William IV's household. Robert was far from overwhelmed by the offer, replying coolly that he wished the salary had been commensurate with the merits of the individual. He was, however, happy to accept, which meant that he was in attendance when the King marched into the House of Lords with his crown on crooked, to dissolve Parliament on the eve of the first Reform Bill. Six years later Victoria had succeeded. She married her cousin Albert of Saxe-Coburg Gotha in the February of 1840, and Melbourne was again Prime Minister and offering his dear Lord Robert the further office of Groom of the Stole to the Consort. Robert could not be unaware that his family's great wealth and consequence had influenced the choice; a petty German princeling was a nobody beside the old entrenched Whig nobility. The pay was £800 a year, he thought it niggardly for what virtually a condescension on his part. Many years later Charlotte was to remark to a daughter-in-law, apropos an invitation to Windsor: 'My dear, we shall have to go, *they* will be missing us'—which neatly defines the attitude of the Whig aristocracy to the Crown.

5

Nel Mezzo del Cammin

If Horace Walpole was disapproving of Moor Park as being too artificial, his judgment on Wharncliffe Lodge was that it was too rugged. (Pope described it as being built on 'rifted rocks, the Dragon's late abode' and thought it a very suitable lair for Lady Mary Wortley Montagu, who he detested.) The legend of the Dragon had passed into local folklore, its origins have been lost. Walpole sneered: 'Old Wortley Montagu lives on the very spot where the dragon of Wantley did, only I believe the latter was much better lodged; you never saw such a wretched hovel; lean, unpainted, and half its nakedness barely shaded with harrateen, stretched till it cracks.'

This had been true enough when Louisa Wortley was writing to Caroline Creighton in 1797, and sending her friend a sample of the offending material. Since then James Stuart Wortley had restored the place, reinforcing the thick stone walls that kept out the weather and replacing ill-fitting doors and windows that let it in.

Formidable parents are apt to produce in their children a strong inclination for a quiet life. Lady Erne, having shaken off her invalidism, and with it the years of foreign travel, was charmed to accept her son-in-law's offer of old Wharncliffe Lodge as a home; perched above an interlacing floor of branches through which the Derbyshire hills could be seen, she was as happy as the birds, her only neighbours. The Stuart Wortley children loved to ride over and visit her, she was never alone for long.

She wrote to Caroline, exiled in London during the Parliamentary Session, of how much she had grown to love her 'cloud-scenery'. 'I am fonder than ever, I think, of the Place, and I am but a *little* frightened at night when I happen to lie awake for hours . . . Your Child (Caroline) found her way *through the clouds* in which I was *literally* enveloped, and surprised me very agreeably, when I considered myself quite sure of no *human* foot approaching my mysterious dwelling. She was amus'd with surprising, and look'd all the better for her ride. It did not rain except for a few seconds whilst she was with me, and she look'd like a flower with morning dew on it.' The Wortleys had this one surviving daughter, and there was the same sort of intuitive understanding between those two as there was between my own grandmother, another Caroline Stuart Wortley, and myself when I was a growing-up girl.

When James and Caroline inherited Wortley they had all the fun of making it habitable, and turning a wilderness into a terraced garden. Not having had to spend his childhood in lodgings abroad, James was the more domesticated of the two. He bred a silky-coated brand of Yorkshire terriers, raised pheasant and partridge chicks which ravaged his wife's flowers, liked attending farm sales and talking about the price of pigs, and had to have two eggs for breakfast every day from his own hens. Lady Granville, who laughed at everybody, was unkindly amused when an attack of gout made it agony for him to put foot to ground and he shot from horseback, the painful foot in a flannel shoe.

They had handsome children, John, James, Charles and Missy (Caroline), the more loved as they had earlier lost two little daughters. His wife he often exasperated but she always tenderly loved him, and their lives grew together, she the ivy, he the oak. And to him she was always 'my dearest, darling Car' as she had been in the early days of their marriage.

Letters are dangerous signposts to characters; it is tempting to accept Lady Granville's dictum about Caroline Stuart Wortley— 'like cool moonlight after a hot day'—and see the characteristics that produced this effect in her every word and action. Still she had, for all I know, no detractors, even Lady Granville, grown waspish years later, was still calling her 'such a love'. Not a clever woman, and not ambitious for anything but her family's happiness which included recognition for her husband's devotion to duty. She feared he might not stand up for himself without her constant support which she prayed might never have to be withdrawn. (She need not have been afraid, she outlived him by eleven years.)

The children were like her to look at, with the same reddish brown waving hair and eyes that had an agreeable trick of looking sleepy while being extremely observant. She adored music and the theatre, and passed on the enjoyment of both to her children. She was nearly always in a state of nervous agitation about health, and feared the stenches of London in summer (cholera breeding), and would send the children away to rural Hampstead when an epidemic threatened.

She had worn only 'short mourning' for her grandfather, the Earl Bishop, but when George III died mad in 1822, ordered full Court mourning for herself and her family. It was generally felt that though he had made enormous blunders in dismissing his Prime Minister Chatham in favour of the Doge's grandfather, the incompetent Bute, and thus losing England the American Colonies, his private life had been all that was decent and moral. Now, 'the weight had gone that slammed the palace door on whores'. As a consequence of repressive upbringing, his five sons broke out in all directions; as Mary Wortley Montagu had once said of a rake, *they went to all lengths.*

The saddest occasion for which Caroline and Lady Erne had again to wear mourning was for the death by consumption in her twenties of the other child of the Evian breakfast party, Eliza Hervey, who had married Charles Rose-Ellis.[1] She died tragically young, as her pretty mother Lady Hervey (who wore the hat with the loops of amber ribbon in the Guttenbrünn painting) had done, and as her own daughter was to do. Lady Erne's sister, Louisa Liverpool, was too *éblouie* with her husband's[2] tactful handling of the trial of George IV's Queen and the praise he had had for it, to mourn as her sister and niece did for the dear little girl who with her cousin Caroline had been sketched by Sir Thomas Lawrence (by now Court Painter) when he was only twelve. Lady Erne was provoked to write to Caroline, 'She (Louisa) writes me the sort of letter which is wholly inapplicable. I am *not* giving way to unreasonable grief, still less to anything like repining; but my feelings were nevertheless deeply wounded and many sad recollections arose to embitter them. I have now seen three persons very dear to me, of three successive generations, sink to untimely graves—any one of whom ought in the common course of nature to have survived me.'

Soon after James Stuart Wortley's election as MP for the Hallam division of York in 1819 (he, as has been said, already sat for the tiny family constituency of Bossinney in Cornwall) it became a necessity to have a house in London large enough to entertain in. The two eldest boys were now at Harrow, Charles the youngest

[1] She was the mother of the 1st Lord Howard de Walden.
[2] Prime Minister 1812–1827.

had gone to tutor, the nursery years were over. James did the house-hunting and started negotiations for a house in Curzon Street, at the thought of which Caroline's heart sank—it was such a slummy neighbourhood for all its nearness to Piccadilly and its great family mansions. If she had to leave Wortley, she would have preferred a house in a quiet Square, or, more daringly, in one of the small white villas linking Nash's classical terraces that were part of George IV's town planning project in healthy North London.

In 1819 she wrote to her mother: 'The house in Curzon Street is ours, dear Mama, £12,000 and a lease of 900 and odd years which will last out many of our descendants. I am hurried and nervous with the suddenness of the decision, the more so as I hate the situation tho' I like the house very much; and that is an end for ever of my dream of a house in a Square or in the Park. But this I must try to forget, and hope I shall grow to like my new house, especially as the Doge is enamoured of it.'

In spite of great neighbouring houses with high walled gardens she feared that the neighbourhood was sadly raffish. As a small boy James had been stolen away by gypsies and not found for two whole days, she never felt safe when her children were out of her sight. About a Charity Ball, of which she was patroness, which was to be held in one of the City Livery halls, she wrote: 'I have no doubt it will be well-filled, much better than at *our* end of the Town, where Almacks Rooms have *hardly time to cool* between one Charity ball and another, and Hanover Square has not the attraction of fashion.' A daub was sold by street-hawkers of a rough party at Almacks, violently coloured, labelled 'Tom and Jerry sporting the toe among the Corinthians at Almacks'. Caroline was however obliged to admit that much as she disliked the neighbourhood, the shops in the arcades in the Regent Street Quadrant were delightful.

The house in Curzon Street is still there,[3] with lawns in front of it, all its original neighbours, Devonshire House, the greater part of Lansdowne House, Chesterfield House, having gone; the street still has the curve of a country lane meandering down to a village market, once muddy underfoot and after dark a haunt of

[3] It was sold to Lord Crewe in 1899 and re-named Crewe House. It was there that James entertained his fellow members of the Owls Club, a literary club so-called because of the late hours it kept.

C*

ruffians and whores—in these two last respects wonderfully un-
changed to this day.

Her aunt, Elizabeth Devonshire, with whom Caroline had always been a favourite, wrote to her from Paris: 'Tell me what you
are about, if you draw or sing, are gay, or regretting the Dahlias
and the high woods, the Simplon, and the thinned sunny walk to
the Greenhouses,' and Caroline could have cried, remembering the
tunnel of rock and fern behind the stables which they had christened the 'Simplon'. However, her happy adaptable nature kept her
always on the windy side of care.

While the moving-in was going on, she wrote from temporary
lodgings in Brook Street to Lady Erne, 'If I did not want to be at
home again, I should completely enjoy myself just now. My mornings are spent at the new House and in shops, and my evenings at
the Play, in Boxes as large as this room. I see my aunt Devonshire
every day, and as she always contrives to have a few men about
her, beside Mr. Clifford and Mrs. Lamb,[4] she has a pleasant little
société.

The widowed Duchess, having been shown the door of Devonshire House by the 6th Duke, lived in rather gloomy grandeur in
a house in Piccadilly. She had had a good life as a *grande
amoureuse*, and was to end it unexceptionably as a patroness of
the Arts, having, like her father the Earl Bishop, developed a taste
for antiquities at a moment when excavation in Rome was gathering momentum. She poured a good deal of Cavendish money into
the excavating of the Forum, and like her father died on good
terms with the Catholic Church and was wafted to bliss by the
prayers of cardinals. One cannot part from Bess Foster, born
Elizabeth Hervey, without a last admiring glance at her. Both in
Angelica Kauffmann's portrait that hangs at Ickworth, and in
Cosway's miniature, she has the face of a thoughtful and scheming
kitten, if such a thing were possible. When powder went out she
let her curls revert to their ordinary brown. The soft glance, the
musical voice, resisted age.

George IV's London was on the surface gay—hysterically so.
Every royal birthday was a public holiday with fireworks. Sydney
Smith, the witty Canon of St Paul's who has been conceded the
last word on his times, gave it as his opinion that the parallelogram

---

[4] Augustus Clifford and the Hon. Mrs George Lamb, the Duchess's two
children by the 5th Duke born before her marriage to him.

of streets lying between the Oxford Road and Piccadilly enclosed more wealth, beauty, and wit, than ever in the history of the world had been collected into a space so small. To people like Lady Erne and Lady Granville London Society lacked *ton*; for so many of those who had contributed to it a glint of genuine wit were gone. The most pitiable wreck to outlast their beautiful world was Lady Caroline Lamb, her life over at forty, living in virtual exile at Brocket, separated from her husband William Lamb,[5] one of the sharp-witted imps of the Devonshire House circle with whom Caroline Creighton as a little girl had played. 'It were all very well,' she wrote drearily, 'if one died at the end of a tragic scene, after playing a desperate part; but if one *lives*, and instead of growing wise remains the same victim of every folly and passion without the excuse of youth and inexperience—what then?' No short life has ever held so sparkling a promise; no life was ever more surely lost for love. Byron's was the image never dethroned in her heart. Those who remembered the Byron of ten years earlier never forgot the delicious thrill of seeing him limp heavily into a London ballroom, scowling like Vulcan while looking as handsome as Antinous.

By 1830 George IV, too, was dead, and no sooner was the breath out of his body but the last mistress, Lady Conyngham, the stout vixen (and her cubs) was out of the Castle with every moveable she could lay her hands on in a string of carriages loaded to the roof.

The younger brother who succeeded him as William IV had a head shaped like an egg boiling over with sparse curls, and was a godsend to caricaturists with his slouching sailor's gait and fund of improper stories. He was quite unlike his predecessor in that he had no taste, no charm, and no looks, where George IV as a young prince undeniably had had all three in high measure. (Sir Walter Scott, an admitted Royalist, wrote of his easy good manners, 'he has the art of raising one's spirits, and making you forget the *retenue* which is prudent everywhere, especially at Court'.)

Once George IV had ceased to animate it, the Pavilion became blameless as milk pudding under the smothering domesticity of Queen Adelaide's rule. But William had more of their father George III's common touch than his brother had had—he liked to

[5] Later to become Lord Melbourne.

please people irrespective of class or kind, showing himself
liberally to them in public. Caroline Wharncliffe became a great
favourite with both King and Queen for the unruffled sweetness
of her manners and her cheerful readiness to be amused. It was
nearly impossible to bore her, though Caroline the younger was the
recipient of some rueful letters from Brighton. After dinner the
King liked to play 'commerce', and undertook to teach it to Lady
Wharncliffe who admitted to being 'very stupid at cards', to which
he said, 'Come, come, Ma'am, you are *fishing for a compliment*,
but you know very well what I think of you, how much I admired
you long ago, do admire, and always shall admire you.' The Queen
and the ladies sat around a table talking about their *fausse couches*,
while Adelaide counted the stitches in her Berlin wool embroidery.

In the midst of the Reform fever of 1831–2, the Doge was
'doing up' the Curzon Street house, painting the rooms—which the
writer's grandmother remembered as darkened by trees—the
colour of fresh cream, 'the difference in the light at the end of the
drawing room in the morning is not to be told'. In June 1826 he
had been offered a peerage, accepted it and taken the title of
Wharncliffe, thus vacating the Hallam division of York county.
Caroline wrote to Lady Erne—'the King was beyond measure kind
and gracious to the Doge at Ascot, and when he told him his last
decision (to take the name of Wharncliffe) approved, but added,
'My good fellow, you will now be the Dragon of Wharncliffe all
the rest of your life.'

James was depressed; things were not going so well in Yorkshire. Times were bad for colliery owners, and the ironworks which
he had inherited gave him much anxiety. Skilled labourers from
the overcrowded South were pouring in to the West Riding, the
blast furnace men, the 'puddlers' who heated the coke to a white
heat, and the 'hammer men' who raked the carbon 'scale' from an
incandescent mass and dragged it in their huge tongs to the 'rollers'
which flattened it to bars and rods and plates for steam engines.
These were taking work from the Yorkshire smelters and puddlers.
Pressure of orders which made the hiring of outside labour inevitable set up much discontent, so that he was not sorry to be out of
industrial politics. The House of Lords had always been looked
upon as a haven of ancient peace and to James Wharncliffe it had
once seemed so; it was to turn out very differently.

No enlightened Tory doubted the necessity of ending the

situation by which the sons of cadet branches of a family—such as the Wortley's Bossinney, or Thackeray's Queen's Crawley—were the inheritors of constituencies returning six members to Westminster. Borough-mongering, the selling by agents of parliamentary boroughs to the highest bidder, was a disgraceful practice, and widely condemned, though High Tories believed—or wanted to believe—that hereditary seats were the only means of keeping gentlemen in Parliament; Wellington thought this. The Aristocracy fitted by birth and fortune to do so ruled the country as by right.

In Disraeli's *Sybil*, Lord Egremont remarks to his mother: 'I should very much like to be in Parliament and particularly to sit for the old borough; but I fear the contest will be very expensive.' 'Oh, I have no doubt,' said Lady Marney, 'that we shall have some monster of the middle-class, some tinker or tailer or candle-stick maker with his long purse, preaching reform and practising corruption, exactly as the Liberals did under Walpole . . . A young candidate with the old name will tell. I shall go down and canvas.' 'I have great faith in your canvassing,' said Egremont, 'but still, at the same time, the powder and shot—' 'Are essential,' said Lady Marney, 'I know it, in these corrupt days; but Marney will of course supply those. It is the least he can do; regaining the family influence and letting us hold up our heads again.'

In *The Member*, an autobiography by a Scot, John Galt, the only novel about the Reform Bill written at the time, the Member, Mr Jobbry, purchases himself a seat which he gets cheap because the session of Parliament is half-way through, partly in order to find gainful employment for a nestful of cousins' children 'all gaping like voracious larks for a pick'. A crony advises him to let it be put about that he has money for the purchase. 'Keep your thumb on the price,' he says, 'and just let out that you have no relish for the clamjamfry of a popular election, but would rather deal with an old sneck-drawer (a manipulator of door latches) than plague yourself with canvassing; depend upon it ye'll soon be hearing of some needful lord that will find you out and a way of treating with you . . . He enquired of what party I would be: and I told him with the Government party to be sure. 'I'll no just say,' quoth he, 'that you are far wrong in your determination, because the Tories have the ball at their foot, and are likely to rule the roost for some years'. 'I daresay they are,' said I, 'but between Whigs and Tories I can make no distinction,—a Tory is but a

Whig in office, and a Whig but a Tory in opposition, which makes
it not difficult for a conscientious man to support the government'.

Mr Jobbry took a gloomier view of it when in 1832 the bill was
finally passed; 'It was not,' he wrote, 'as other changes that had
taken place before, a mutation of the Tory party among themselves,
but a total renunciation of that ascendancy which they had so long
preserved, and during which they had raised the country to the
pinnacle of glory. I had, indeed, a sore heart when I saw the Whigs
and Whiglings coming louping, like the puddocks of Egypt, over
among the right-hand benches of the House of Commons, greedy
as corbies and chattering like pyets (magpies). It was a sad sight;
and I thought of the *carmagnoles* of France . . .'

The French Revolution was much in people's minds during
1830 and 1831—in the Wharncliffes' case delightfully crowded
out by young Caroline's marriage to a clever lawyer, who was to
be a dearly loved son-in-law,[6] in the August of 1830, followed by
that of the youngest of the Wortley children, Charles, to Lady
Emmeline Manners, daughter of the Duke of Rutland. The eldest
son, John, had been married since 1825 to Lady Georgiana Ryder,
daughter of Lord Harrowby. Emmeline Manners was shy, abrupt,
classically beautiful.[7] Caroline, with her loving heart, determined
that there should be no stiffness between her and her youngest
son's wife—admittedly, not easy to fit in to the family scene.
Charlie was conventional, an officer in the 10th Hussars. All that
is remembered of him is his classic brush-off to a London hostess
'the Tenth don't dance', and a remark about hunting treasured by
his family, uttered in fun but in all seriousness too—'the nesty
stinkin' violets are comin' up everywhere and spoilin' the scent'.
It must have been a love match, for two more unlikely people
never vowed a lifelong attachment.

Caroline wrote to her mother: 'We get on amazingly well with
our new daughter. She is a very nice creature and will, I think, suit
us all, especially (when) we get her out of some old habits of
indolence and irregularity about hours, etc.' Emmeline—a poetess
with 22 volumes of poetry which she intended to publish after
marriage—was such an interesting character that she merits a note
to herself.

To Jem in the March of 1831, his father wrote gloomily about

[6] John Chetwynd Talbot, fourth son of Charles, 2nd Earl Talbot.
[7] See Appendix.

Lord John Russell's proposals for reform of the franchise.

Curzon Street.
You have all of you treated me for some time as such a croaker as was not to be listened to; my worst fears are now to be realised, and the blow inflicted upon the Constitution has already made it stagger . . .

The existing form of representation, he realised must be changed but the idea that this could only be done by placing the franchise in the hands of the middle classes and sweeping away at a blow all nomination by family influence in the hereditary constituencies of 'close Boroughs', filled him with gloom. He feared 'an excess of popular feeling in the House of Commons' (popular speakers to him meant stirrers up of trouble among the working class, the sort that Mr Jobbry likened to the *carmagnoles* of France). 'It (the Bill) is so contrived as to flatter and feed the vanity and self-sufficiency of the Middle classes, and therefore to make them clamorous for it; while the Radicals and the mob see in it the certain step to the consummation of all they want and wish for. When I say *mob* I mean the turbulent part of the lower classes, for I am not sure whether in those classes there are not more real supporters of the Crown and the Aristocracy than in the class immediately above them. If then the bill is thrown out, no one can be blind to the risk to which every establishment in the country is exposed. Nor have we any government—or rather any set of men to look to to form a government—which could withstand this plague if the present Government was to go out . . .'

Go out it did, and dramatically. Tory families recalled their sons from the Continent and the Universities in order to put them up for family constituencies at the Election which—if his ministers succeeded in persuading William IV to exercise his royal prerogative and dissolve the present Parliament—must come.

April 22nd, 1831, was to be the fateful day; the second reading of the Reform Bill had been passed by a majority of one after a debate in the Commons lasting seven nights. James Wharncliffe now gave notice of an address to the Crown against dissolution, for the longer Lord Grey's Government remained in office the more chance there would be of amending the Bill.

London was thought to be in danger of serious rioting. Wellington put up the iron shutters at Apsley House, Lord Dudley in Park

Lane took the glass out of his windows and barricaded them with deal boards. At his house in Staffordshire, Himley Hall, precautions were taken to fend off incendiarists from Birmingham. Older people like Lady Erne remembered the grinning *sans culottes* of Paris brandishing knives, the women with aprons-full of stones, and heard with terror of Cabinet Ministers' coaches being overturned in the London streets. Much of it was exaggerated.

All the afternoon the venerable House of Peers buzzed like a trodden-on wasps' nest with argument and conjecture, until a distant thudding turned into the sound of guns—the King on the urgent recommendation of his Ministers was on his way to dissolve Parliament.[8]

He entered the Chamber with his crown on, which he ought not to have been wearing at all as it had not yet been officially confirmed to him. On the return journey he hung half out of the coach window to return the goodwill of the crowds who loved Royal Billy with expansive waving. The Lord Mayor ordered the city streets to be lit with set-pieces of coloured lamps, and flags were hung from every window. Only the houses of those who opposed Reform were dark. The Doge, to whom public speaking did not come easily and who had to nerve himself to do it, had only just stood up to speak on his motion against Dissolution when the King arrived. It hardened his resolve to put forward a more moderate point of view as soon as Parliament should reassemble.

Caroline Wharncliffe wrote to Lady Erne a few days later: 'Unless you were in London, dearest Mama, you can have no idea of the state of excitement and busy idleness in which we live, and the difficulty therefore of finding half an hour to write in . . . John (her eldest) is animated to a degree you never saw, and trots in here four or five times a day to report what he has heard. Jem (her youngest) is gone to Scotland to try either for himself or John, that

---

[8] A note in the Ebury papers from Sir Frederick Watson is dated April 22nd, 1831, to Robert Grosvenor, recently appointed Comptroller of the Royal Household: 'I hear (but not officially) that the King will go to the House of Peers this day at $\frac{1}{2}$ past two o'clock. The Comptroller usually attends upon such occasions. Robert Grosvenor told a friend that he actually heard the King say, when his Master of the Horse told him that the State coach could not be got ready at a moment's notice, that the matter was so urgent he would go in a hackney cab. This, however, did not prove necessary. But it took so long to turn out the Guard that he was met by it on the return journey.'

the latter might remain here, ready to go down to Bossinney, or be in the way for anything that might occur in Yorkshire. It is evident from *The Times* that the Whigs are not quite confident, and find it necessary to make great exertions.'

Next day she wrote again: 'You will be glad to hear that we escaped without broken windows last night, tho' we were stout and would not light one candle. We all dined at the Dundases,[9] and a party of us went in the Coach and drove all about the most frequented streets, thro' mob and all. There was very little noise, but many windows were broken in different parts of the Town. We (in Curzon Street) were only treated with hisses and groans, and a lamp at the gate was broken. John's house escaped. Several of the clubs have behaved gallantly and in consequence had every window broken. There never was such a humbug illumination, no enthusiasm, no violence, except window breaking in which Boys are as much or more concerned than men.[10] John's just come in and says we are beat at Dover! Hélas, it is a bad beginning but no great surprise. . . .'

One gets the impression that a good deal of fun was being got out of the situation. London Society was indulging in one of its recurring *crises* of silliness, as was to happen in our own time during the General Strike of 1926, when political dinner parties were held secretly in the hope of bringing members of the two parties together—the sort of private and exclusive parties at which really crucial decisions on policy are always supposed to be made but so seldom are. In 1926 political hostesses were thinner on the ground than in 1831, but there was a similarity; the political string-pulling of Wimborne House and Londonderry House did not affect the issue.

James found an inflammable situation in Yorkshire that autumn whither he had gone to address his Yeomanry. His appearance at

[9] The Doge's sister Mary Stuart Wortley had married William Dundas, MP for Edinburgh.
[10] The King was indignant to hear that stones had been thrown at the darkened windows of Apsley House where the Duchess of Wellington lay dying. Caroline wrote to her mother—'So the poor little Duchess of Wellington is gone at last! I am told she suffered but little, and was latterly so happy at the Duke's kindness and attention to her that she said she never knew what happiness was before. I am glad for his own sake, as well as hers, that he did his duty by her at last. I hear he sat up with her the last night.'

Doncaster Town Hall was received equally with applause and with hisses, to which he replied as soon as he could make himself heard that he would not tolerate either favour or disapprobation, and proceeded to *cayenne*[11] his refractory yeomen till they were silent. He told them that if any of them did not choose to continue serving under him they were at liberty to retire, nothing would induce him to resign the commission entrusted to him by the King, simply because his political views happened not to agree with their opinions. In fact the Doge showed that he too had a lot of Yorkshire in him.

The rejection by the Lords of the second reading of the Reform Bill should have inflamed the London crowd whose feelings had been worked on by Radical agitators, but no houses were set on fire. Caroline was nervous, but in her own words 'stout'. In the early hours of October 8th James Wharncliffe moved his amendment to the Bill which was rejected by 41 votes. Next morning's newspapers announcing the defeat of Reform were bordered with black.

Caroline wrote to her mother: 'The hour at which I got into bed this morning and it being Saturday, prevent my writing you more than a few lines, just to give you the pleasure of knowing we are all well and safe notwithstanding our fatigues and the threat of disturbance. There never has been the least violence, and even this morning at *sunrise*, when all those who would have formed a mob were up, we left the House of Lords as quietly as if they had rejected a Turnpike bill, and with no more people round the doors. This is a curious fact.'

Moderation was creeping in. During the debate Lord Dudley called the Bill in its present form an instrument of self-destruction, likely to unleash rioting in the industrial Midlands where he himself owned coal. From October 1831 to April 1832, James Wharncliffe with the same thought in mind worked to get the bill to be acceptable to both parties. His own two constituencies of Bossinney and Hallam were now represented by his son John and he held out against the clauses that disenfranchised all pocket boroughs of less than 2,000 inhabitants. After long deliberation he accepted the necessity as a concession to public feeling if not to private good.

He found a rather nervous ally in his co-father-in-law, Lord Harrowby. There were many meetings in Lord Harrowby's house

[11] Family slang meaning to 'pepper'.

in Grosvenor Square (where the Cato Street conspiracy in 1821, to seize and kill all members of Liverpool's Cabinet while sitting over their wine after dinner, had been at the last moment discovered and prevented).

Wharncliffe saw clearly that the ultra-Tories by refusing to admit the necessity for *any* measure of reform would force Lord Grey into a Coalition with the extremists of his own party. He and Harrowby were nicknamed 'the Waverers' for their un-Tory behaviour and received abusive and even threatening letters which frightened Caroline. Wharncliffe wrote to his son Jem from Brighton in the January of 1832—'We dine at the Pavilion tomorrow for the first time, but with what sort of Party, God knows. Lord Grey is to be there today, with, as is surmised, a list of new Peers to be submitted to His Majesty, and among them are said to be included *all the Bastards*,[12] by way of a bribe, I suppose, to induce him to consent to making the others. But I will not believe all this till I see it. Some Peers, perhaps 10 or so, may possibly be made. Lord Grey must know that there is no disposition on the part of many who opposed the last Bill in the House of Lords to throw it out again merely because they cannot approve of the principle, if they can obtain alterations in the details. An attempt to overbear the Peers would be a most wanton destruction of the authority and respect of that branch of the Legislature. But the friends of the Government talk coolly of it as necessary to the future support of Government . . . If they can reason thus, we are indeed delivered over to the blind and the Reckless.'

We, who in our own time are so accustomed to seeing men of straw created peers to bolster up the party in office, can hardly imagine the chagrin suffered by the hereditary peerage at this prospect. It shook the very bastions of privilege.

Lady Wharncliffe wrote to Lady Erne on November 24th, 1831. 'I suppose, dearest Mama, as you sometimes see *The Times*, you were surprised by a paragraph lately alluding to a negotiation between Lord Grey and our Lords W. and Harrowby. It is very true, but as I thought it would not be very agreeable intelligence to you, I felt in no hurry to write about it.[13] The state of the case is this. The Doge, thinking that it would be a great thing if some attempt at conciliation were made before the bringing in of the new Bill,

[12] William IV's children by Mrs Jordan, the FitzClarences.
[13] Lady Erne was an unrepentant Tory and abhorred Whiggery.

determin'd to see Lord Palmerston (Foreign Secretary), with whom
he had a very satisfactory conversation, so much so that he (Wharncliffe) desired him (Palmerston) to tell Lord Grey that if he had
no objection to communicate with him, himself, he should be very
ready to wait upon him whenever it was convenient'.

Lord Grey *was* interested, and asked for a résumé of the proposed amendments.

Caroline wrote to her mother: 'Yesterday the Doge had a long
interview with little Johnny Russel [*sic*.]. Very satisfactory.' But it
was not to be so simple. Lord Grey was performing an extremely
hazardous tight-rope walk between his Ministers, the entrenched
Tories and the red-hot Reformers. Lord John Russell, 'the little
Napoleon of Reform', the terror of borough-mongers, had one
more ace up his sleeve. If the younger sons of Whig noblemen
were to be created peers, and possibly some industrialists of respectable antecedents, the gap of forty-one votes by which the Bill had
been turned down on its first reading in the Lords, could be closed.
The King indignantly refused—even the tempting offer of peer-
ages for his bastards would not budge him.

The Waverers (they were aptly named, for during the winter
of 1831 and the Spring of 1832 they appear to have wavered away
from supporting the Bill only to waver back again in its favour),
might have secured for themselves a note in the history books of
the future had they been more forceful and less upright men. The
bulk of letters exchanged between them make heavy reading, they
are so well-meaning, so honest and so dismally repetitive.

Disraeli hammered the Waverers remorselessly in *Coningsby*
and must be quoted: '. . . .scared at the consequences of their own
headstrong timidity, they went in a fright to the Duke and his able
adviser (Lord Lyndhurst) to extricate them from the inevitable
results of their own conduct.' His comment is that while the Whig
ministers might have made terms with an audacious foe, they
trampled on a hesitating opponent. 'The truth is, the peers were in
a fright. T'was a pity; there is scarcely a less dignified entity than
a patrician in a panic.'

In the tense week of May 20th, 1832 the third reading of the
Bill was passed by a majority of nine. At the fateful third reading
everyone concerned with the event, and there were few who were
not, crushed into the Gallery of the old House of Lords to hear the
Waverers put their case.

'The Governor,' Caroline wrote to her mother, using the children's favourite name for their father, 'was as stout as a lion, and roared with eagerness but not with temper, and made a capital defence for himself and friends generally.' Wellington followed, dissenting with pain and concern from his two friends, Wharncliffe and Harrowby. He refused to consider that the Bill, even in an amended form, could strengthen the Legislature. Whereupon Lord Grey resigned and the Duke, who with seventy other peers had left the House of Lords in protest, was recalled by the King to form a Government, which he failed to do. The King reluctantly agreed to create a few new peers to break the deadlock. In June the Tory lords, overborne, withdrew their opposition, and on June 7th, the Reform Bill received the Royal assent.

By the time the dust had settled Tories might have asked themselves what they had been afraid of, Radicals what they had been fighting for. No revolution was ever effected more painlessly. In the committee stages many of the recommendations of the Waverers and their supporters were to be quietly adopted.

James Wharncliffe, conscious of a coolness towards him among his Tory peers, and seeing now no prospect of Cabinet rank, spent his time improving Curzon Street, and sailing a new boat between Chelsea and a villa they had taken near Hurlingham. It was a relief to him to get away from all the gossip about political personalities. Here Caroline used to join him when London got unbearably stuffy (she craved for air and would stand on the beach at Brighton inhaling draughts of it), but she did not want, even to please him, to be for long out of the delicious 'swim'.[14]

As time goes on the Doge begins in character to appear more like his looks as painted by Sir Francis Grant. Her portrait (in her fifties now) by the same artist makes her look contented, stouter certainly, also a little bit sleepy, in a black lace shawl. In his he is sitting sideways, his elegant legs in tight trousers strapped under the foot, crossed, his eyeglasses drooping from one hand, one arm resting on an elegant writing-table. Under the chair is one of the silky Yorkshire terriers he bred. What strikes one is the earnest gentleness of his expression, and the muddle of papers, mostly letters, all about him. A cane waste-paper basket of a trellis pattern absolutely brims

---

[14] From time to time James lent the villa to friends, once to the diarist Charles Greville who spent a fortnight there with his current mistress. James had some ado to keep this from reaching his wife's ears.

with them. We know he was a patient lengthy correspondent.

His public life, however, was not over. During Peel's Ministry two years after the first Reform Bill Caroline was writing to Lady Erne: 'I hope, dearest Mama, that you will not be unpleased to learn that our fate is *sealed* and that we are *in Office*.[15] I am much provoked to find that he has no privilege of *franking*, or any other that we can think of. I have, however thought of one that concerns Myself and which I value as it deserves, which is the carriage *entrée* at the Drawingrooms. I cannot say how I have always envied *that* advantage. When he (the Doge) kiss'd hands today, the King (William IV) said to him, "I can never forget what I owe to your family", and in presenting him with the Seal added, "I cannot hold it in my hand, but long may it remain *in yours*," alluding to the weakness of his hands and the great *weight* of the Seal, which is solid silver, as we learnt when the Doge brought it home.'[16]

In the December of the same year, 1845, James Wharncliffe suffered another attack of gout that had plagued him for years, but this time with an alarming difference. Their father's gout was something of a joke with his children, seeming as it did to occur whenever he wanted to avoid Caroline's sometimes indiscriminating sociability; it seldom interfered with his daily visits to the House of Lords. He was by now a familiar figure in debate, a dry precise speaker but to be relied on for a certain dogged honesty that would not let a debating point be lost sight of.

In the January of 1842 Lady Erne died. After a poor start in life—an unhappy marriage, wretched nerves, unremitting anxiety about money—she sailed, and the comparison to a small wind-buffeted craft is not unapt, into sunny waters. There was such sympathy between her and Caroline that one could picture the other in any company at a given moment. Writing from Paris Caroline would say, 'I am very glad you like your bag. We see you exactly in the evening with bag, fichu, and fan, in the drawing-room at Ickworth, and I saw you also exactly sitting sola-sola, very snug and quiet in the bookroom, beginning your letter to me.' The Doge took charge of the funeral at Wortley. He wrote to his wife in Curzon Street:

[15] Lord Privy Seal. Perhaps she intended the pun!
[16] James Wharncliffe was divided in his mind both on the issue of Reform and on that of the Repeal of the Corn laws, his honest heart and legal training inclined him to see both sides of every question.

'January 18th, 1842.

'We are now just returned from the funeral, and poor Gooma [the children's name for their grandmother] now rests where I am sure she would have chosen, but from her utter want of selfishness which made her averse to giving anybody any trouble on her account. How soon will that vault be open to receive *me*? A few, a very few years, at all events will see that day. May I be prepared for it . . . God bless you.'

He had become Lord President of the Council in '41, in the ministry formed by Peel after the defeat of Melbourne on the question of imports on corn and sugar. He looked forward to going down to Windsor to attend his first Council Meeting. Caroline described it in a letter to her daughter: 'the Queen was good-humoured and civil [not by any means always the case] to them all; and enquired of the Governor after you and me, very graciously. They lunched first, and after the Council were told to amuse themselves as they liked till five o'clock, in which interval several of them walked to Eton to see their sons or grandsons, and Eddy[17] walk'd back with the Governor to the Castle. After five they went out driving or riding with the Queen, and dined at night.' To walk to Eton and back across the fields after a Council meeting, to ride out in Windsor Park with the tireless little Queen, to dine and play whist with the Prince Consort after dinner and then stay up listening to Wellington's campaigning anecdotes till after midnight, made up a strenuous day for a man not in the best of health.

As Lord President James Wharncliffe had to prevent, with all the legal weight at his command, the lay Tory peers from voting to uphold the sentence on O'Connell, the detested Irish member, who was under arrest on a charge of conspiracy against the Government. O'Connell had held, in defiance of a Government proclamation, a meeting at Clontarf near Dublin calling for the immediate repeal of the Corn Laws. His trial was a farce with a suborned jury. Greville wrote: 'The high Tories and their press are exceedingly indignant with Wharncliffe for having interposed to prevent the lay lords from voting and over-ruling the Law lords.' James was unperturbed by unpopularity; he had been through it before in '32.

In mid-June 1845 the hay was washed out and the corn threatened. Worse, the potato crop both in England and in Ireland

---

[17] Son of John Stuart Wortley and Georgiana Ryder, later to be the 3rd Lord Wharncliffe and 1st Earl.

became mysteriously diseased. There would not be enough corn to
spare from the sodden fields of Britain to feed the starving Irish,
and no potatoes, the staple food of the Irish peasantry. Peel, a
Free Trader at heart, made the great decision of his career, the
decision to repeal the Corn Laws,[18] supported by the Whigs (now
Liberals), but feeling that the temper of his Cabinet was not with
him, resigned in the December of 1845.

Jem Stuart Wortley kept his mother, who was entertaining
house-parties in Yorkshire, well supplied with political gossip and
family news. He was by now the happiest of men, Jane Lawley,[19]
who had kept him in suspense for five years, having accepted him
in November. Her parents, Lord and Lady Wenlock, had a house
in Berkeley Square, only a step away from Curzon Street, so that
he could be with his Jane while keeping an eye on his father, who
would insist on going down to Westminster in spite of the pain
in his leg. When he was unable to leave his bed, the Doge's
friends would call on him with the rumours that were circulating in
political circles, which caused in him an agitation of mind hardly
conducive to recovery. Greville was told by him that Peel had
always intended repeal, provided he could do so with unanimous
Cabinet support and that his resignation had been a tactical move.

Jem's happy letters reassured his mother. The Wenlocks were
going down to Torquay for Lord Wenlock's cough and his father's
doctor assured Jem there was no reason why he should not go too.
He wrote to Caroline from there on December 18th: 'My own
Jane is looking more beautiful than usual, and is radiant with happiness and contentment. Under these circumstances politics have
lost some of their interest to me, notwithstanding the crisis . . .'

That very same morning news came by special messenger that
the situation in Curzon Street had worsened. Jem caught the next
coach and was in London by midday, sending a note by hand to
his brother John who had gone to the Talbots in Kent. 'I send this
to you by the quickest method I can devise to beg of you to make

---

[18] It was going to be impossible to feed Ireland from England, equally
morally impossible to let the Irish starve for bread with foreign corn
waiting to be admitted at the English ports. The Anti-Corn Law League
that hit at privilege and monopoly was gaining recruits every day. Not
for the first time in English history weather was the instrument of
radical change.

[19] Daughter of the 1st Lord Wenlock of Escrick, near York.

known to Caroline (their sister) the sad news that it must convey—
namely the very great danger in which our father lies here. You
are aware how unwell he has been for some time past . . . the
(doctors) have just left him, telling me, alas! that it is all but
hopeless. It appears to have been a stroke of apoplexy which
struck him in his sleep—I fear that my mother cannot be up before
tomorrow evening, and what then? God grant that she may not
find all over. What will she do? How will she bear it?'

The black-edged note that met John on his arival in London
told its own tale: 'My mother alas! cannot be here till between
7 and 8. She knows nearly the worst from the express which I sent
her by the mail train last night but still I dread the consequences
of such a shock . . .'

So at the end none of them were with him; their grief was
made heavier by the absence of a last word or look. The blinds in the
Curzon Street house were pulled down, a hatchment carrying the
arms of Wortley was hung on the iron gates between the lamps,
one of which had been broken during the week of Reform.

Greville, who had complained in the past that Wharncliffe
could on occasion be cold and distant in manner, wrote with unusual warmth that no man ever died with fewer enemies, with
more general goodwill, or been more sincerely regretted by those
who had regard for truth and honourable conduct in public life.
The Queen wrote to Caroline unaffectedly regretting the loss of
one she had known for so long.

The fear Caroline had always had that she might go first was
removed from her. She was now sixty-six. She had married for
love and, though they had had their sorrows (the loss of two
little daughters in infancy and very recently the loss of their son,
Charles, from the after-effects of a riding accident), the long sun-
shiny stretches were what she remembered, going back to the days
when they were first married and Zac, as she called him then, was
still in the Army and expecting to be sent overseas. She had stiffened herself to be brave as befitted a soldier's wife, thinking he
had already sailed and would probably be killed at once, when a
carriage drew up to the door and there was a thundering knock. 'I
felt sure,' she wrote to her mother, 'it could be nobody *but* him, yet
I still doubted my happiness. However, I was not long in suspense
for I believe he took but one step from the chaise into the room!'

6

James's

1832 was a political watershed and, for the researcher through family documents (myself), another kind of watershed. Amused, nostalgic, charmed, one plays a sort of game with one's more remote ancestors, moving them about, not manipulating but easing them along in their chosen directions. Until there comes the moment when the long shadows they cast touch oneself, and with a soft shock of recognition the children and grandchildren of Charlotte and Robert, Caroline and James, are seen to have substance because they are (or were) within the living memory of people one knew. In the preceding chapter the descriptions of the passage of the Reform Bill are first hand, my mother's grandparents lived through it. She, avid like myself to know more about the days before yesterday, asked questions endlessly. In late life, growing deaf and blind, she wrote down what she remembered, finding that memory which must begin and end with oneself can never be depended on, and that good breeding dictates reticence. Also by the time she was of an age to be talked to, life was becoming more crowded with events that preoccupied her elders—earthquakes, wars, famines, revolutions—brought to the breakfast table to be read by everyone and made explicit by lurid illustrations in *The Illustrated London News*.

The watershed of 1832 was a personal happening to my mother's family. (It was still referred to in my childhood as if it had happened only a couple of generations back instead of nearly a century.) My grandfather Norman had absorbed William Morris's Radicalism but more because he had come under the spell of Morris himself than from a compulsion to man barricades. His mother, Wellington's niece, had been a high Tory and married into the Grand Whiggery that had ruled England under the four Georges. By the time of my own mother's birth Whig and Tory as political definitions had been replaced in the case of the Wortleys and Grosvenors by Disraelian Conservatism and Gladstonian

Liberalism. Life was more expensive and more crowded, rooms more crammed with furniture, clothes more lavishly trimmed, shops more plentiful and grand, streets more jammed with traffic, all hurrying them on into the next century.

1845, the year in which James Wharncliffe died, was the turning point of the Victorian century, the year of the repeal of the Corn Laws, of the Chartists' renewed demand for a People's Charter conferring universal suffrage—'one man, one vote'—of Faraday making his first electrical demonstration to the Royal Institute, of Hudson the Railway King, of Newman's being received into the Roman Church. From now on the term 'Victorian era' is applicable with its implication of a new dawn breaking. In his Victorian essays the historian G. M. Young has written of the years that immediately followed:

> In 1850 Huxley is twenty-five; Bagehot twenty-four; Rossetti and Meredith a year younger; Lewis Carroll and Leslie Stephen are eighteen; Morris, Acton, and Du Maurier are sixteen. Behind them, as schoolboys, Swinburne, Morley, Pater; Hardy is just ten; and over them all droops the fading youth of Matthew Arnold in the full decrepitude of twenty-eight.
>
> Painters, poets, journalists, reformers, scientists, novelists, but no mention of architects unless you count William Morris, already beginning to look critically at what was being done to ancient buildings in the name of progress.

Jem, the youngest of the children of Caroline and the Doge, became a lawyer. His letters to his mother about his first brief, his first offer of a constituency (Halifax), his first speech in the House of Commons, are irradiated with natural gaiety and optimism. Like her he was musical, loved the theatre (and the leading ladies in it), was ready to carry on the family tradition in politics but not to take it too seriously. It was the Doge who felt he had to put the brake on: 'Bad and precarious as the trade of a politician has always been, it has now become ten hundred times worse than ever, and holds out to a younger brother nothing but Poverty and disappointment. Let me beseech you then, my dear Boy, not to make a shipwreck of your prospects upon that rock ...'

His children, who regarded their 'Governor' as the arch-prophet of doom, listened to his advice, and in the manner of the young disregarded it. In the September of '45 James was writing excitedly to his mother from York where he was on Circuit, having been appointed Attorney General for the County of Durham, which was a stride forward in his career, and also a step in the direction where his heart lay.

He had met Jane Lawley in Paris in the October of 1841 at a party at Lady Granville's, whose husband's term as Ambassador there was coming to a close. James, who was perfecting his French, was rather at a loose end and the Wenlocks were glad to have the company of a fellow Yorkshireman. If it was love at first sight with him it was not so with her. She was a tall girl of twenty-two with delicate yet strong features, and eyes that, from shortness of sight, seemed to stare through you and beyond. After the first meeting they did not meet again for a year, when he followed her to Paris where her parents were again staying, proposed marriage and was refused with an abruptness that shocked him.

After that another two years went by before he dared to speak to her again. The Wenlocks respected their daughter's reserve and did nothing to press the match. If mutual friends praised him to her, she withdrew into the wounded silence which is the refuge of sensitive hearts. However, in his letter of September 1845 he had said to his mother: 'Thank God! My confidence in myself has been restored and I have again placed myself at Miss Lawley's disposal, with, I hope, better chance of success. Nothing can be kinder than Lord Wenlock who is evidently anxious for my success and he and Lady Wenlock (with their daughter's knowledge) have given me permission to go over and see her as often as I wish which, of course, is everyday.' He had, however, to warn his mother not to get on to her high horse and gallop away with the idea that all was settled. Courtships, when marriage was a life contract, could not be hurried.

The happy ending must be told even though it is to go back a little in time. On November 18th, 1845, he was writing from London: 'Thank God! My dearest Mams, all is now settled and I am a happy and accepted lover! They arrived in Town last night, and this morning I went by previous arrangement to receive her decision from her own lips. I feel that I have secured a treasure beyond price and I look forward with delight to the devotion of my future life to the study of her happiness. I am going to dine in Berkeley Square (the Wenlocks) and we all go at 9 o'clock for her first sitting to Grant[1] for her picture. About ½ past 10 I hope to see my father come in to Berkeley Square where he will be received with every cordiality. It is manifest that they are all, father, mother, and brothers really delighted.'

The Doge described the meeting to Caroline, detaching his thoughts from the Cabinet meetings which he was obliged to attend in spite of the pain of 'gout' and the swellings in his feet and hands which made it hard to walk or to write a letter, and wrote from the Privy Council Office: 'I did not arrive in London till past 9, as the train was near an hour after its time at Derby. Upon my arrival I found a note from Jem telling me that his affair was quite settled, and that we were at liberty to announce it to everybody. I take for granted he had written you this comfortable intelligence. He added that he was to dine at Lord Wenlock's at ½ past 6, after which they were to adjourn to Grant's for her to have her first sitting, and to return to Berkeley Square by ½ past 10, when he begged me to go there, which I did, was admirably received, and remained there till near ½ past 12. I took the young lady by surprise and kissed her hand when I first went in, which she took very quietly.'

Jane Lawley's quiet manner, which concealed shyness, concealed also a resolute will, inflexible standards of behaviour, and great personal courage. She passed on her looks, her height, and the distant gaze of her short-sighted blue eyes to the writer's grandmother, her daughter Caroline.

In a month from that happy evening, the Doge was dead. After so long an engagement, it was agreed that mourning should not be allowed to interfere with Jem and Jane's wedding, which took place in the following May in the halcyon Spring of 1846, when the trees of Nuneham Park which had been lent to them for the honeymoon were in full summer leaf. Caroline modified her mourning for the occasion, to resume it over the next ten years that were left to her, for her sister Mary Dundas, for her much-loved son-in-law John Talbot, and, saddest of all, for her eldest son, dead of consumption in 1855, a year before her own death.

[1] Sir Francis Grant PRA. This portrait was to be Jem's wedding present to his bride. He had first admired her riding in the Bois in Paris. Sir Francis would do preliminary sketches in his studio; in the finished picture she would be riding a white horse of the blood of the Godolphin Arabian.

She took on the lease of the Dundas' house in Lower Grosvenor
Street. (Wharncliffe House in Curzon Street had become John and
Georgie's.) London suited her she said, her favourite treats, music
and the theatre, being close at hand. She was beginning to feel her
age and was too stiff now to garden; besides it was so handy for
the grandchildren. She had a great many of these: John and
Georgie's five—Edward, Francis, James, Mary and Cicely; Charles
and Emmeline's Henry, Archibald and Victoria; John and Caroline
Talbot's Gilbert and Edward; Jem and Jane's Archie and Charlie.
The last named were to have five daughters, all remarkable women
(still held in loving memory by my generation) but none to their
sorrow remembered *her*, for Caroline Wharncliffe died in 1856
when Mary and Margaret were tiny, and Blanche, Caroline and
Katherine were not yet born.

Jem, who had been Recorder of London under Palmerston, then
Solicitor General,[2] was tipped to be the next Speaker. Ten years
after their marriage, Jem, when out riding with his Lawley
brothers-in-law, was thrown on to the highroad. He was never a
good horseman and was besides a tall and heavy man. Because
Jane was just recovering from a confinement the brothers agreed
that she must know nothing about Jem's fall; she never forgave
them for it. He put up with the pain of his back for nearly a
month, never letting her see how much it hurt him, until the pain
became too severe to be any longer hidden. For a long time he was
extremely ill.[3] He revived but as a changed man, no longer his old
optimistic self. From family letters it is seen that this change in
him from sunshine to darkness terrified the children.

Years later a daughter was to set down: 'I cannot write of the
long miserable years when between bouts of illness there were
sometimes months of apparent recovery when hopes rose high,
only to be crushed again. At last, somewhere about 1869, all efforts
to stand and walk and be as other men, were relinquished, and
from that moment the clouds seemed to lift. He suffered less, he
took up as it were a new life within narrow limitations, and his
natural bravery and serenity of mind made for years the sunshine
of our home.'

[2] He was Judge Advocate General and a Privy Councillor in Peel's
government in 1846.
[3] Modern medical opinion gives it that he had broken his back, hence
the ensuing paralysis.

Once bound to a wheel-chair, Jem reverted to his natural sweetness of temper, and for the remaining twenty-two years of his life did not utter a word of repining. He had always hoped to be Lord Chancellor. He had been Solicitor General in Palmerston's Government of 1856, but was to hold the office for only one year before his accident. The Speakership of the House of Commons was kept open for him for some weeks during the illness that followed, in fact for an unprecedented length of time, until it became obvious that he was not going to be able to accept it.

Jane did not leave him by day or night during the worst weeks and months of his illness for more than an hour or two. He came to depend on her step, her voice, her touch. Sheltered as all Victorian women of her class were, she had never had any dealings with money, but when Jem could only raise an arm with pain to scrawl a feeble signature and reading hurt his eyes, she took upon herself the sole management of their affairs. As he could no longer practise law, the house in Carlton Gardens had to be sold.

There was an interim time when they moved to Richmond, but as the two girls were growing up, and the boys had to be educated, something in the way of a London home for them had to be contrived. The house they chose, No. 16 St James's Place, is, I fancy, no longer there or has been absorbed into another building, though some of the houses in that delightful cul-de-sac that runs from St James's Street to the Green Park, happily escaped the bomb that completely obliterated Samuel Rogers' house in the last war, dispersing into empty air the echoes that hung about it, the voices of those who frequented his famous breakfasts.

'James's', as the young Stuart Wortleys always called it, was tall and narrow, looking down onto pavements and a mews at the back. It had nothing to recommend it but its cheapness and the fact that it was accessible to all the London Clubs and therefore to Jem's friends. It was like a rookery densely crowded by active talkative young birds. Jem's condition necessitated three menservants to carry him up and down the steep staircases and to push his bath chair out in the Park. Nothing about 'James's' was laboursaving.

Old friends found it convenient and pleasant to drop in from Brooks's, from White's, from the Travellers', and the Athenaeum, to talk and listen to Jem who regained with his serenity his lively critical sense of humour. All in all, the house fulfilled its purpose very well, and there were relations only a few streets away, the Wenlock grandparents in Berkeley Square, the Wharncliffes in Curzon Street.

The girls grew up, the boys went to Oxford, Jane somehow contriving not to run into debt. The children, of course, knew that money was scarce but having simple wants, were not oppressed by the fact. 'Everything in those days was a joke,' one of them wrote, 'even our mother's fits of anxiety and depression. What miles we walked, laughing by the way! Omnibuses did not exist then for such as us and the family carriage was kept mainly for our father's use. But an occasional cab fare had to be found and a minimum number of penny stamps, and now and then the butler would refuse to finance us any more in these matters and his "book"—a dreadful document—had to be taken for liquidation to poor Mama.'

Mary, the eldest, yearned to be an artist, and at that time the only art school open to women was the Slade School attached to University College, in grimy Bloomsbury.

'As usual when it was a question of serious benefit for any one of us, my mother found the money for a two year's course,' she wrote, 'and so for many months I went to and fro from St. James's Street to Bloomsbury at the cost of much effort for others as well as myself. I had to walk and afterwards stand at my easel all day, perhaps with feet already tired and aching from the dance of the night before.'

'At that time no young woman of quality could be seen alone in the streets without scandal. Cabs being expensive, the schoolroom contingent had to be called upon as escort. If I was to get to the Slade School in good time it must be persuaded to take its morning walk inconveniently early; and the schoolroom party, though headed by the most good-natured of governesses, refused firmly to walk all the way to the further end of Gower St. with me, and later fetch me back again. A middle course had to be found (Mama helplessly winking at it) and it was established that if my protectors would take me through the danger zone of St. James's and Bond St. and across Regent St., I would face any wild beasts that might lurk in Mortimer St. and Tottenham Court Road by myself. The only danger was the disgrace of being seen there alone. As I hurried guiltily along, my heart would thump at the sight of a cab laden with luggage. Who might not be inside it? As it crawled slowly by the inmate would have ample time to recognise me. How glad I was when it rained and I could hold my umbrella as a shield. If it was fine the only thing to be done was to turn my back on the thoroughfare and gaze with absorption into the window of a shop for second-hand clothing . . . Coming back after the day's work the process had to be reversed and I walked until I got within range of a shilling cab fare. It was a very tired girl with very muddy feet who crept thankfully into an old four-wheeler and hid herself in a corner of it for the last mile home. Then in the winter dusk, when I looked into the sittingroom on my way upstairs, there was the dear patient old father on his sofa, saying, "Oh Mary, I have been waiting for you! Do make up the fire." He had been brought up as he would say "at the pit's mouth", and in the old home at Wortley, lying high in the bleak moorland country about Sheffield surrounded by coalfields, the big grates used to blaze with Wharncliffe Silkstone coal wellnigh all the year round.'

Mary Stuart Wortley, the only one of Jane's daughters to have no dress sense at all, must be allowed here her say on the subject of dress about which she was extremely didactic, though to her great-nieces, of which the writer was one, she looked a hopeless frump, having early on refused to wear stays 'for reasons of hygiene'. Her hats were somehow square and like footstools, her shoes were elastic-sided like those of the Dame in a Pantomime. She thought poorly of my generation's spirit, and we found it impossible to imagine *her* as the intrepid Slade student, splashing through the mud of Bloomsbury.

'The dreadful crinoline,' she told me, 'became general when I was a girl [in the late sixties] in the schoolroom. Always some kind of stiff petticoat was worn to puff out skirts to the required crinoline shape. Usually this was of white cotton highly stiffened with starch, but it was often made of *crin* or horsehair, a very harsh thick material. When some genius invented a skirt which could be made of any light material stiffened by three or four rows of flat ribbon wire run round it at intervals, it was hailed with acclamation. It kept its round shape so beautifully and kept the skirt so well out of the way of muddy heels. If I remember, it was of quite reasonable proportions at first, but presently Fashion made it her toy and it grew enormous, balloon-like, horribly inconvenient.' (It was also very draughty!) 'Woman is now known to

D

be a bi-ped. In those days the fact was quite successfully concealed, as any dual garment except of the smallest and most flimsy kind was forbidden to her. Skirt upon skirt had to be piled on. The unfortunate inmate was therefore little more really clothed than the clapper of a bell!'

(Dear Great-Aunt, how well I remember you when skirts became unbecomingly short, how trenchantly you expressed yourself, shrivelling what small rag of vanity I flew by glancing pointedly at my exposed legs! Our elders sometimes mentioned that you had had a great deal to put up with in your life; now that I know what this circumlocution implied, I wish I had known you better.)

When she was over thirty Mary Stuart Wortley married Byron's grandson, Ralph King, Lord Wentworth, later to be Earl of Lovelace, son of the poet's daughter Ada: a risk from every point of view. He had been married before, not happily, and had a daughter whom he refused to accept as his. Mary was emerging from a long hopeless love-affair when they met. Ralph was different from any other man she had ever known, a dedicated mountaineer, a mathematician like his mother, and behind him lay the romantic shadow of his grandfather, Byron. No Victorian young lady could have been insensible of this.

Mary, most mistakenly, took pride in the exercise of an uncompromising commonsense, the sort of pride that invariably precedes a fall; she brushed aside the Byron heredity, which she thought of as a tale of old unhappy far-off things, best forgotten. Loving Ralph, she thought she could bring him to this point of view. He was never to escape his heredity and the failure of his first marriage had dried up the springs of affection in him. He valued Mary's bracing absence of 'cant' and her honesty, and thought, if indeed he ever gave the subject consideration, that they could have a satisfactory *mariage blanc*—perhaps never knowing that she had married him for love. After a year or two he began the prolonged stays away from home from which he seldom wrote to her. Her letters to him, begging for news, always stop short of a plea to him to return to her; so much is not mentioned, or is skirted round, and by him ignored. After one of his frozen silences lasting for three days or more, during which she had tried by every means to thaw him, he would take her hand, press it, saying 'I forgive you, Mary'.

Turning over family letters, I find one from Jane Stuart Wortley written about two years after this marriage when, after enduring Ralph's silences and absences, Mary had gone away by herself 'to think it all over'. Jane Stuart Wortley was as nearly a saint as anyone need be, but she was of her 'world'. She wrote: 'Without for a moment contending that you have not all that you may justly claim, I do strongly think that you still have a great deal. You have fairly tried your plan and it has done some good. You ought now to stay at home. You must not bring yourself into the position of being the gazing-stock of all London. Think of the indelicacy of such a theme in the foul mouths of a London club. One foolish word might start all that now. You must throw yourself into his pursuits, enter into his pleasures, keep up to his interests. Be self-controlled, distant if you will, but whether it be the Byron papers, astronomy, or any other mortal thing, go into it with him as Anne[4] does. Whatever comes later you must stay now, at all events long enough to *keep off Season-gossip.*' (My italics.)

Jane, who had heroically allowed Mary to brave the perils of being recognised by her acquaintances in the Tottenham Court Road, and was to demonstrate in her old age a remarkable ability to adapt by learning to use a typewriter when her eyes were failing, when presented with emotional behaviour so far astray from the norm could only talk about 'Season-gossip'. Mary, however, was not impervious to that particular argument, though it is unlikely that she believed men's clubs to be dens of profanity and obscenity, having seen too much of her father's old friends when they dropped in at 'James's' on their way to and from White's and Boodle's.

She returned to Ralph, and from then on made *his* way of living and thinking her own. When he decided, with pain and distaste, to put into print the facts about Byron's love affair with his half-sister Augusta Leigh, and thus vindicate his grandmother, Lady Byron who had brought him up and whom he adored, Mary stood by him. Her private and not at all favourable opinion of Lady Byron was never voiced. An astute observer in the family has said: 'If there is anything to be learnt from the history of the *affaire* Byron, it is the danger of mysteries and partial disclosures.' Ralph felt that the only way to lift the cloud of censure from his grand-mother's memory, and in a roundabout way to explain if not to

[4] Ralph Wentworth's sister, Lady Anne King, married to the poet Wilfrid Blunt, another difficult husband.

condone his grandfather's conduct, was to set it all down truth-
fully in a privately printed book.[5] His wife wholly supported him,
secretly bored by the whole subject but always on the side of
perfect candour.[6]

Sad to relate after all those muddy walks to Gower Street, Mary
was never to succeed as an artist. In some autobiographical notes,
never finished, she talks about the overlong apprenticeship of Slade
students under Sir Edward Poynter to drawings from 'the Antique'.
Her brother, Archie, also a pupil of the Slade and later of the RA
Schools,[7] with far more talent, rebelled against the Ruskin ultra-
academic approach to painting as too time-consuming as I was, two
generations later, to discover for myself.

'I, on the other hand,' Mary wrote, 'was a little too subservient
to Poynter, whose powerful draughtsmanship I admired. Many
were the arguments, long and furious, between Archie and me
about our different ideals of art. There was but a year between us;
all our lives we had practised drawing together, and planned and
fought without ever a real quarrel or a bitter moment.'

This was in the seventies when the fixed planets in her sky were
Morris and Burne-Jones (Mary is one of the descending damsels
who all have the same faces and figures, in the latter's 'Golden
Staircase'). She veered to the delicate hybrid art of Walter Crane,
poised between the Pre-Raphaelite and the Art Nouveau.

Had she been a man she would have been an artist-craftsman
after Morris's own heart. Because of her husband's long absences
from home, the management of the Lovelace estates, Ockham Park
in Surrey and Ashley Combe in Somerset, fell to her. She taught

---

[5] *Astarte: The Facts about Byron and Augusta Leigh.*

[6] I hope she drew some comfort, she had had little enough affection
from him in her marriage, from his dedication to her of *Astarte* : '—in
acknowledgment of steady sympathy and encouragement, and equally
necessary criticism, without which this anxious duty, impossible to
neglect and hardly more possible to execute, could perhaps neither have
been undertaken or carried through.'

Trenchantly she set down after his death her opinion of the whole
sorry fable : 'Perhaps it would have been better never to publish anything about Lord Byron when he was dead; but after a heavy accum-
ulation of coarse misrepresentation, the dark night of his real history
seems less suffocating than the poison of flatteries and familiarities in
apocryphal compilations.'

[7] He founded the Society of Portrait Painters, and was President of it
till he died.

herself to be a very fair architect; the studio she built herself was not for painting in, the table would be spread with plans for the drainage of tenants' and labourers' houses. She was for a time a pupil of Voysey who was a family friend, and was allowed disastrously to remove Hawksmoor's arcaded loggia from Ockham and replace it with something vaguely Dutch and, I seem to remember, partially thatched. Mary Lovelace passed fearless moral and aesthetic judgements. The late seventeenth century panelling of the hall at Ockham dating from an ancestor, Lord Chancellor King, was pronounced to be wanting in sincerity, so out it went, and with it much fragile pretty furniture, lumped together as bric-à-brac. In came the products of the Arts and Crafts movement of unpolished wood, uncompromising in their plainness.

The portrait at Ockham of Byron as an Albanian brigand caused Mary Lovelace to utter a short sigh of exasperation whenever she looked at it, though she excused fancy dress in her sister-in-law, Lady Anne Blunt, who wore it with more reason since she was an Oriental scholar and spent much of her life in the East. Mary lumped all dwellers in the near and far East together under the title of Obadiahs: she was of that dismissive turn of mind.

A race of interlopers known, but never clearly visualised, were the objects of her particular scorn: 'Vague middle-class heathens who don't go to church and don't dress for dinner.' They were said, also to waste water which was needed for the land by having unnecessary baths. Bathrooms she cryptically announced 'led to mésalliances . . .' She and Ralph were utterly opposed to plumbing; one of my earliest childhood memories is of being woken in the night by a sound of something thumping near my head; it was the 'night soil man' replenishing, with clods of earth, the privy next to the nursery, in which you pulled a rope and earth descended with a terrific rumble. But this was just one of the less attractive aspects of Ockham, like the green parrot who was allowed, even encouraged to tweak my pigtails. Aunt Mamie's white cockatoo, William of Ockham,[8] would sidle along the tops of the tall dining-room chairs, nipping the backs of our necks as it went, the brute! These birds were to Mary, her children, her joy, her relaxation. I wonder now what Uncle Ralph, who had repudiated his own child, thought about his wife's many nieces and cousins who came

---

[8] Named by my father for the mediaeval philosopher. After 27 years he laid an egg; this lapse was hushed up.

and went at Ockham. My mother wandered into his library once, aged about twelve, looking for something to read. He pushed a first edition of Burton's *Arabian Nights* across the table to her and told her to sit down, read it, and not talk. He, who was such a bad husband and father, was most tolerant of any young person who shared his interests, though in general showing frantic intolerance towards his guests, who might not smoke except after dinner in a fireless smoking-room, or stay too long, or laugh too loud. In this he shared a characteristic with Robert Ebury's mother, Marchioness Westminster, who was so mean that 'she resisted the strongest hint of even her best friends to stay with her for four days who had only been invited for three.' This sort of behaviour threw Ralph into such a rage he would retire to bed and refuse to get up till the guests were gone.

Had she married a gentle easy man, no doubt Aunt Mamie (as we called her) would have had her softer side brought out, she would not have been so ferocious about the middle classes or so dogmatic about art. She would not, on the other hand, have been such fun. I like to think that she was a link with the eighteenth century for she remembered her mother's mother, Lady Wenlock, taking her to visit an old Grenville aunt and their solemnly curtseying to each other. Lady Wenlock had been Caroline Neville, granddaughter of George Grenville, one of George III's Prime Ministers (and possibly the most incompetent of them all). She remembered stories of family parties at Stowe when the descendants of the 'Mighty Seven', Lord Grenville's children, arrived in huge lumbering *carosses* of ancient design drawn by six horses, with children and grandchildren, nurses, attendants, grooms, all easily to be accommodated in the great house—the forebears of Lyttleton, Grenville, Fortescue, Williams-Wynne, King, Proby, Camelford, Stanhope, Leveson-Gower, St Germans, Beaufort, Egremont, Sydney, Grandison, Egerton, Temple, Nugent, and Kinloss. Like a vast spider's web with filaments invisible yet tougher than the toughest steel, all these relationships spread and multiplied, throwing, through marriages, a network of fine glittering strands over the whole of the British Isles, enclosing Society in its seemingly imperishable web.

When Ralph died (he was found lying on the garden path, looking no longer grim but satisfied as though he had just worked out a problem in higher mathematics), his widow drew on a lifelong habit of self-discipline to conceal her heartbreak. 'Mary is being so good and brave,' one of her sisters wrote to another, 'behaving so like a lady—you will know what I mean.' I know exactly what she meant. Excessive tears and loud lamentations were only indulged in by the lower classes. 'Don't make that noise, child,' I would be told. 'It is like the maids. Only servants cry like that.'

With Ralph's death a brake on Aunt Mamie was removed and she turned into the powerful arbiter of manners which I and my cousins remember. She died during the last war, extremely angry when bomb-blast broke the panes of one of the Ockham green-houses.

The household at 'James's' had begun to be depleted before Jem Stuart Wortley died. Inevitably Margaret married first. She was her mother over again in looks and bearing. Every garment she put on looked elegant, even the unbecoming tin armour surprisingly worn by her in the character of a Valkyrie at the famous Devonshire House fancy dress ball in 1897 (surprising, because she was by nature hopelessly vague and indecisive and terrified of horses). She was from the moment of emergence from the schoolroom, a Beauty; too good it was thought, to throw herself away on a second son, as she proceeded to do. In 1877, during her engagement to Reginald Talbot,[9] in one of her characteristic letters to her sister in which she laments and contradicts herself over many pages, she writes that she fears her engagement may have to be a long one as Lord Shrewsbury can only allow them a thousand a year. Reggie was in the Life Guards, was ADC to the Queen and was to have distinguished commands abroad, including a Colonial Governorship. As a very young lieutenant he had been sent to America as an observer on Sheridan's staff, and had been present during the final phase of the American Civil War.

Margaret was as good a musician as her brother Charlie; in a letter she heroically declares herself to be resigned to a life of 'penury and Scarlatti', Chopin and Mozart presumably being only for the rich. She was to be painted in Paris when Reggie was Military Secretary there, by Carolus Duran and by Jacques Emil Blanche, to be 'poetized' by de Montesquiou (the Baron de Charlus of Proust), to be dressed by the great Worth, who called her *la plus pure type Anglaise, d'une beauté inoubliable*—never

---

[9] Son of Henry, 3rd Earl Talbot and 18th Earl of Shrewsbury.

descending from her altitude of beauty (half-smiling, head slightly inclined) till she sat down at the piano to play Chopin, when all indecisiveness left her and the music flowed from her fingers as I have not heard it do from any others.

It has always been a regret that, to me at least, the gift of making music has not been handed on. The only great uncle whom I can remember was a strict and admirable pianist in the class that would now be called professional : my grandmother's brother Charlie.[10] He was a shy man, thick-set, always conventionally dressed in a dark suit, not to me the romantic figure that he must have appeared to Carrie Millais, when he was a young widower with a baby daughter. Carrie, his second wife, was the youngest daughter of the painter, and she fell in love with, and—it has always been said—proposed to him. He did not love her but they had music as a bond. She was such a strict musician that she would not play to give and get pleasure until she had practised the piece for days. Elgar, who could not abide amateur pianists, would rather have heard her play than any professional. He worshipped her in a dreamy ethereal sort of way, called her his 'Windflower', and wrote one of the *Enigma Variations* about her. The Violin Concerto of which she was the inspiration was headed with the Spanish words *Agui esta el alma de* . . . . here is enshrined the soul of . . . . (the four dots representing her initials, Alice Caroline Stuart Wortley).

Archie Stuart Wortley had, after leaving the Slade, become a pupil of Sir John Millais. It was through him that Charlie had been drawn into the Millais orbit. Lady Millais, who had been Effie Gray, Ruskin's wife, was regarded with fastidious distaste by my grandmother and great aunts; she was a very dull woman with whom they had nothing in common. When Tommy Grosvenor died in St Petersburg leaving Sophie a young widow, she lived for some time at Moor Park until she met Albert Gray, Effie's younger brother who had been a page at Effie's wedding to Millais. Subsequently Albert and Sophie married. I remember him as a very tall benign person, chiefly interested in Hakluyt's *Voyages*, about which he would talk to me as if I were a fellow scholar. Distinguished older men had a delightful habit of talking thus to the very young. It is this sort of communication without condescension

[10] Charles Beilby, created Lord Stuart of Wortley in 1916. His first wife was Beatrice Trollope, niece of the writer who had died when their daughter, Bice, was born.

that I remember of Henry Newbolt, of whom I shall later write, of George Trevelyan and W. P. Ker.

One of the now vanished by-ways of London was Trafalgar Square in Chelsea where the Albert Grays lived, in a house called Catherine Lodge. It had been built by a speculator—and what unerring taste they had!—at the end of the eighteenth century, and had a country feel to it. I remember it opening with French windows onto a country-sized garden with borders of irises and huge shady trees. There were in my London childhood many houses of this sort, not large or splendid, not to be canonised by posterity, just simply countrified; where it was possible to have a game of croquet on the lawn or tea in the shade, or to play brigands in the bushes; from whose ground-floor windows floats the sound of a piano on which is being played the *Clair de lune* of Debussy, or a young voice singing Verlaine—*Le ciel est par dessus le toit*, set to music by Reynaldo Hahn, while men from a delivery van in the road outside are carrying gilt chairs into the house for an evening party.

When he thought I was old enough, Uncle Charlie gave me a photograph of the Guttenbrünn painting of the breakfast party at Evian, carefully explaining the relationships in it and exactly where I came in the family tree.[11] It was not until years later that I learnt of the distinguished public career which brought him the peerage which he is believed to have accepted in order to satisfy Aunt Carrie's social aspirations.

Charlie died in the April of 1926, two days before Elgar was to conduct the London Symphony Orchestra at The Queen's Hall in his First Symphony and the *Variations*, for one of which Carrie had been the inspiration. He wrote to her: 'It was a great ordeal. I missed something too great to express—I looked at the familiar seats and my eyes filled . . .'

Often, in my grandmother's drawing-room, he played for me. When old Grosvenor House, and the whole area as far as and including Park Street where the Eburys lived, was sold to become a mammoth hotel, Caroline Grosvenor was given another house on the Westminster estate, No. 2 in the same street at the Grosvenor Square end. It was a little slice of a house, now swallowed up by the American Embassy. Where it had been possible at No. 30 to

[11] As the great-great-granddaughter of the little girl with hair cut *à la Jeanne d'Arc*.

D*

enjoy garden sounds, at No. 2 the noise of the traffic was appalling. Its frail old windows shook, the very frame of the house trembling with it. But when the thick interlined curtains of green silk were drawn on the crowded little drawing-room, with its grand piano and a Burne-Jones painting of naked nymphs disporting themselves among rocks, it had miniature grandeur. Once at tea-time, Uncle Charlie having just replaced on the table one of those brown china tea-cups of ample size which were a reminder of the days when my grandparents enthusiastically fostered the Arts and Crafts movement (they went with the de Morgan tiles in the fireplace and the lustre plates), Caroline said to him, 'Play something, Charlie, something of Norman's for this child.'

So he wove together for me the airs to which my grandfather had set the nursery verses of Robert Louis Stevenson. When my own granddaughter asks me to pick out one of Norman's settings for her, I am once again leaning against Uncle Charlie's knee, watching his big hands with clean square nails drawing music from the keys, so that the shaded Chinese lamp making a circle of light above my grandmother's woolwork and the kind face above me, enclose me again in the safe world of childhood which my grandchild still inhabits.

For a long time Charlie and Caroline had been collaborating over the publication of Stuart Wortley letters covering more than a century, from their great-great-grandfather the Earl Bishop up to their father Jem Stuart Wortley, the whole giving a picture of a landed family from the time of the French Revolution, through the Regency, the Reform Bill, the industrial unrest in the north, the accession of Victoria and successive Parliaments.[12]

When Charlie died Caroline finished *The First Lady Wharncliffe and Her Times* alone. Though she had written fiction she had very little interest in the why and how of History. 'My brain feels stiff and sore after a day of poring over papers,' she said, 'I long to be in my studio, painting.' The tiny room she called her studio at the very top of No. 2 Upper Grosvenor Street, looked out over roofs at the back of the house; a view which most London houses used to have, of soot-bitten eighteenth century brick and rain-streaked nineteenth century stucco, with far down below a cobbled mews

---

[12] My father, who was Charlie's nephew by marriage, wrote in a memorial foreword: 'He did not grumble at change, but he was jealous that the memory of the older world should not be lost.'

and coachmen's cottages. Caroline used to say that she preferred to keep Christmas alone in London—'then there is nobody about and I can spend all day painting in peace.'

Near me as I write is a water-colour drawing of her, painted at Naworth by George Carlisle, her lifelong admirer. She must have been just married to my grandfather Norman, and looks reluctant at finding herself, so newly a bride, under scrutiny, her eyes exactly matching the blue of her artistic smock (Jane, her mother, had that same blind blue stare). I shall not be as real to my grandchildren as she is to me.

She had suffered a crippling loss when Norman died. Her face had a guarded sadness, her smile when it came sweetened but did not irradiate, 'As though,' as Virginia Woolf wrote of her own mother, 'she heard perpetually the ticking of a vast clock and could never forget that some day it would cease . . .'

She designed a bronze headstone for Norman's grave in North-wood churchyard, an angel with wings and arms outspread before a barred door. The symbolism eludes me; I know if I could find the key to it it would tell me much about her. The technique of modelling in plaster, to be ultimately cast in bronze, was new to her—she took years to master it.

Now when I think of her—and of how with infinite tolerance and love she saw me through the process of growing up—I am appalled by what a little bore I must have been, grinding on to her about social inequality, about God, about my wanting to be an actress, about the conspiracy on the part of Providence and my elders (in collusion) to prevent me from enjoying myself in my own grubby introverted way.

With what patience Caroline stitched at her birds and flowers while I read my verses, feeble imitations of *The Idylls of the King*, for the most part, or derivatives of the Georgians, Alice Meynell, Frances Cornford, Kathleen Tynan. Truth obliged her to tell me that my efforts were not poetry, but she softened the blow by stories of how fierce Tonks had been to her over her first attempts at painting at the Slade School. She had persevered and the result was good.

Caroline, like most of us, had a double standard; as an artist she believed profoundly that self-expression in the arts was of paramount importance, as a Victorian she was undeviating about marriage being a woman's duty and the only career worth following.

The two in her case had been happily compatible. Ford Maddox Hueffer wrote in his autobiography: 'Brought up in the back rooms and nurseries of Pre-Raphaelitism, which for better or worse held that to be an artist was the most august thing in life, I learned that the profession of the arts and the humaner letters was in theory a priestcraft and of itself consecrated its earnest votary.' Caroline believed this with all her heart but doubted the practice of the theory. An artist-cousin on the Talbot side, Constance Lane, who strenuously proclaimed freedom from the conventions and did not marry, caused our great-aunts distress for her thinness and shabby shoes. Art (as a profession) and financial insecurity went together in their minds, something one would not wish for one's own daughter. It must have cost Caroline something to let Susan marry my father, John Buchan, or would have if her friends, Henry James and Arnold Bennett, had not assured her that the young man would make his name in the world of letters. To paint and write and sculpt in a non-professional way within the safe circle of marriage was what she had done and was what she wished for me.

From her I got the impression that 'suitable' marriages, that is, marriages within the framework of a class, had a way of working out for the best, for she could produce so much incontrovertible evidence to prove it. All the Stuart Wortley sisters, she, Margaret, Katherine, Blanche, had made unworldly marriages with younger sons, while Mary with courage and commonsense had redeemed hers by taming Byron's grandson, proving thereby how irresistible is the power of a good woman. They had been poor as girls, had had to trudge through mud, and trim and retrim their hats. Their beautiful fearless mother who looked so well on a horse, had given up her life to nursing an invalid husband and, when herself blind and crippled, was pushed about in a bath chair by the village idiot, fearless to the end and satisfied with her lot.

There was in existence (but now no more) a circular painting of these five young women, clustered round a piano, where Margaret is playing Chopin and swaying to the beat. Behind her stands Blanche, ardently listening, and beyond her Caroline, already a widow, in black, to one side Katherine, the youngest of the family, leans on the piano, thinking of something else, possibly of Neville Lyttleton whom she married, while on a low stool in front Mary, the eldest, sits with her hands clasped round her knees and her back to the viewer.[13] The painting has disappeared, but even in reproduction it captures the height, grace and good looks of those five sisters all of whom I remember and called 'aunt' though they were in fact my great-aunts, and my grandmother—the girls of 'James's'.

[13] Probably, as she is the only faceless one, she was the artist.

7

Conformers and a Rebel

The Grosvenor grandchildren, Bertie, Hughie, Alice, Francis, Susie, Marnie and Rosamund, the children of Bo, Norman and Algy, accepted the incomprehensible prejudices of their elders, as children do, without question.

Care was taken to avoid the just wrath of Auntie Siss which was easily aroused, to keep well out of his Lordship's way (did he wear his top hat in bed, they wondered), and to listen politely to their grandmother's Bible readings, while longing to escape to their tree-house in the delectable Wilderness, or to Mrs Mundell the gardener's wife, who gave them tarts baked in saucers with skimmings of cream from the dairy.

Later—very much later—they put together in a privately printed book the things they remembered and had loved best about the house, the garden, and the servants; their adult recollections chiming together like counterpoint in music.

To Caroline Stuart Wortley, youngest but one daughter of Jem Stuart Wortley, who married Norman, the youngest of Charlotte's children, the most impressive aspect of life at Moor Park was the meek way in which five sons and two unmarried daughters spent the day in each other's company, sat for three lengthy meals round the dining-room table, at night received their bedroom candlesticks from their father, retired to finish the day talking in front of their bedroom fires, and all without rebelling.

'I had come,' she wrote in *Moor Park, Some Recollections,* 'from a large uproarious family, closely packed together in a moderate-sized London house, and at first I greatly appreciated the calm sense of space, of dignity and orderliness.

'His Lordship thoroughly enjoyed his position as head of his little kingdom. It would be difficult to find a character in every way more unlike his than that of my mother-in-law. While the key-note of the one was *laisser faire,* the key-note of the other was intensity of feeling—intensity of loving those she admitted to her love—intensity of will to live up to her own high ideal of life. She hated the solidity, the grandeur, the burden of which fell almost entirely on her frail shoulders. She longed for freedom; freedom to hear music, to play with children, to kneel for hours in church, or sit up with a dying woman—yet she was always in her place at meals or punctual for any of the small functions and ceremonies which so pleased and amused His Lordship and were so infinitely tedious to her.'

The transformation of Robert Grosvenor, who in his younger days had been a rake, into a Low Churchman who wrote letters on the revision of the Prayer Book to *The Times*, and was fond of small niggling economies,[1] is hard to accept. His granddaughter Maudie (Glyn) thought him far shrewder than anybody ever gave him credit for being.

She told me that when she first really remembered him he had begun to be exclusively interested in just seeing how long he could keep alive, and that rather obscured his native good sense. He had lived a full and interesting life, had been much liked—'*a wild young man in the highest fashion of the day!*' He was wonderful on a horse, she remembered him at the age of seventy-five pounding the Grafton field on one of her father's hunters. 'I don't feel,' she wrote, 'that I knew much about him. His daily drive; the many topcoats which he wore one over the other according to the weather; his inconvenient habit of hearing anything one said which he was not meant to hear; prayers read in a rather quavering voice toward the end; tall, very sparse, very neat; to me a lay figure.'

This was the easy charmer to whom Lady Cowper had written reams of political gossip, the elegant courtier of Leslie's Grosvenor family group, doomed to be remembered by his granddaughters as having his chin always buried in a starched necktie, mildly annoying their grandmother by being flirtatious with their girl contemporaries in a perfectly proper way. They thought him a terrible snob.

The word 'snob' can have many shades of interpretation. It followed the eighteenth century's blistening perjorative 'toad eater' or 'toady'—literally one who eats toads, and who having swallowed the poison of contempt returns the poison of flattery and subservience. The crudest sort of snob hung about the fringes

---

[1] When Charlotte was dying she said to a granddaughter: 'If I get better, do you think his Lordship would let me have a new chintz in the Drawingroom?'

of Society thinking he could fawn his way into it, for as most great people had debts, importunate mistresses, or ne'er-do-well sons, the opportunities for blackmail were endless. Society, however, had a way of closing its ranks on the outsider. The Earl-Bishop was an art snob; Lady Jersey, the Prince Regent's mistress, was as vulgar a snob as any half-pay Captain's wife condescending to an apothecary's widow. Lady Granville, herself not immune from *de haut en bas* snobbery, was captivated by Caroline Wharncliffe's contentedness with the station to which she had been born and found this a rare and admirable *trait* of character.

In our day, where to have an educated and what used to be called an upper-class accent lays one open to the charge of snobbery and of being almost personally responsible for the 'guilt' of Empire, behaviour has declined and good manners with it. Robert Ebury may have been exclusively interested in his own narrow world but his manners were beautiful; he would stand hat in hand while talking to a woman from the village gathering sticks in the park, using the same courteous address to her as if she had been one of his guests.

If he struck his granddaughters as a snob it was because he had his place in an aristocratic world so small that it was impossible not to be related to everyone in it. It was in its way tribal, and had its trivial loyalties and taboos, and a whole sub-language of nicknames and jokes. I think that my great-grandfather as he grew older simply found it too dull to talk to anyone outside this related circle.

The Moor Park visitors book was almost entirely filled with the names of relations; disentangling them with the help of an ancient Debrett, I find that 'cousin Billy Chesham', who was enormously fat, was the father of the two lovely Cavendish girls with whom all four Grosvenor sons in turn thought themselves in love: Georgie, who married the second Earl of Leicester of the 18th century creation and was thus the sister-in-law of Henry Coke of Longford who had married Katherine Grey Egerton, daughter of the second Earl of Wilton who was Robert Ebury's elder brother; and Katherine, who married Robert's nephew, the first Duke of Westminster, as his second wife. Katherine Coke's half-brother, Seymour Egerton, was a most persistent visitor at Moor Park, as was 'Cousin Dudley', twenty-fourth Baron de Ros (a peerage that zig-zags confusingly through the female, whose aunt, Olivia de Ros, had married Charlotte's brother, the first Earl Cowley). Complicated as it looks, it was clear as daylight to them, and had to be clear to me or I would never have managed to pick my way about in the conversation of my elders.

Of all the visitors to Moor Park who came and went, some of them so often that the servants knew their individual tastes as well as those of their employers, the most frequent and most welcome was Charlotte Ebury's sister-in-law, Lily, wife of the Dean of Windsor, Gerald Wellesley, Charlotte's youngest brother; 'the miserable little being' whom the motherly Duchess of Wellington adopted after their mother bolted from their father with Lord Anglesey.

Queen Victoria adored the Dean to whom she wrote every day (in the heavily black-bordered envelopes which I still have). She had leant on him for comfort during the dreadful year after Albert died, for dependence on a man was essential to her and Gerald Wellesley accepted it as his Uncle Wellington had done. Lily Wellesley (her lovely name had been Magdalen Montagu)[2] was one of those Victorian women mention of whom would be followed by a sigh and a smiling shake of the head, for her beauty made her a legend in her time. Her death broke the mould, for she had no daughter, and her only son died young.

She deserved a better fate than to marry a cold Wellesley, for she loved to be gay, even naughtily so. She told a niece that there was no tense of the verb '*amo*' that she had not conjugated.[3] She and her dry scholarly husband lived in different worlds. After his death she moved to a small house in Farnham, surrounded by more rare and delightful objects than I as a small child had ever seen crowded together in one room. She was very old by then and bedridden, wearing a lace bed-cap. I thought a carved bear painting a Swiss landscape on a tiny easel so desirable that I had to bite my tongue to prevent myself from saying so and tears rushed into my eyes.

Children are acute to tones of voice, the way my grandmother's

[2] She was the daughter of Lord Rokeby, a peerage now extinct, and was Maid of Honour to the Queen.
[3] It was a *secret de Polichinelle* in the Grosvenor family that the boy, who died early, was not the Dean's. No one spoke of it but it was an accepted fact that his father was Charlotte's eldest son (Bo) to whom Lily stood in the relationship of aunt-by-marriage. The eighteenth century's calm acceptance of 'children of the mist' persisted far into the nineteenth.

voice softened as she said 'Lily' held a world of love. When
Charlotte Ebury died, Lily took my mother's hand (she was only
six) and led her upstairs to the bedroom in the Park Street house
from which, in *caelo quies* at last, Charlotte's cabined ample spirit
had escaped. 'She held my hand tightly and talked in her ordinary
voice. She saw no reason for the gruesome whispering so terrifying
to children which are supposed to be a sign of sorrow and a tribute
to the dead, yet she had loved my grandmother with a love passing
that of most sisters, and mourned her, never ceasing to talk of her.'

Caroline found that steering her way among the religious con-
victions of her in-laws was like navigating a narrow channel full
of sunken rocks in stormy weather: 'All the younger male members of the family, who went to Church but mocked impartially at
High and Low practices, were open free thinkers. I think it was the
High Church element (Charlotte and her daughters) who made
the discussions of any subject even remotely connected with
religion unsafe. His Lordship would have been willing enough to
live and let live, contenting himself with mildly chaffing his wife
and daughters. Even the regrettable opinions of his sons never
caused him to lie awake or otherwise ruffle the calm of his existence.
He contented himself with praying for them in the course of
family prayers, always when the subject was present and kneeling
with his elbows on one of the red leather Hall chairs in a peculiarly
defenceless position.'

The day to day existence of the Ebury family had no *style*, the
splendid house in no way influenced its inhabitants. Family prayers,
read by his Lordship with all the servants present except the
youngest kitchenmaid who had to stay behind in the kitchen to see
the breakfast dishes were kept simmering,[4] took place in the Hall
beneath a gallery presided over by figures in grisaille by Sleter. At
the Gallery's four corners were great lanterns of gilt wood and
glass by Robert Adam. From this vantage you looked down on a
family who made no attempt to dress or behave as if aware that the
setting was extraordinary; a perceptive granddaughter says that as
a child the Hall seemed to her limitlessly vast, trying to describe
it was like trying to describe a landscape. Which, in a way, it was;
an indoor landscape opening on tantalising glimpses of the antique

---

[4] Before the introduction of electrically-heated plate-warmers it was
impossible to combine full attendance at prayers of both family and
servants with having hot dishes at breakfast.

world. However, if you had to live in it, it was perhaps best to look no higher than the billiard table and the harmonium at which evening hymns were sung.

It seems to have been a house one had to get out of either to drive donkeys round the Park, along the avenue of great pollarded oaks, or to walk to Rickmansworth or the nearer Batchworth Heath to take a Bible class, or in Victoria's case to practise with her choir. She was a true musician, as was Norman—Charlotte having brought music into the family from the Wellesleys. In a hot summer the house was pleasantly chilly, while outside the garden blazed with an intensity that none who remembered it could ever find words to describe.

There was no need for Charlotte and her daughters to walk to their 'poor peopling', since the stables and carriage horses were at their disposal, but this they insisted on doing. It was one of the ways in which Victorians embraced discomfort to salve their consciences. I have a faded and yellowing photograph of the Avenue at Moor Park and seen in middle distance the bulky forms of the Misses Grosvenor in crinolines and sealskin jackets plodding toward the village where the cottagers, seeing them coming, would hurriedly be setting out the family Bible on the kitchen table.

'An imperious personality kept under iron control—she really had what many claim, iron self-control.' This, let slip by a granddaughter, illuminates my great-grandmother for me, like 'the quick sharp scratch and blue spirit of a lighted match'. 'Oh dear, what a loveless family it was,' she goes on. 'Though I well remember the celebrations both of their Golden and Diamond weddings, I cannot recall having at any time seen Grandmama and Grandpapa walking or talking together. Always the length of the Dining Room table between them, always the vexed question of the windows, opened by her, shut by him. Once, and once only, she talked in my hearing of her youth, in that wonderful deep voice of hers—sitting rather bent in her chair, absent-mindedly stirring her large cup of weak tea. She spoke familiarly of *le Roi de Rome*,[5]—and told of her early married life at Eaton and of the shattering boredom of life there, "doing woolwork endlessly" (that footstool for the Chester Bazaar, "every stitch counted"!) and just waiting for the men of the family to come in from hunting and shooting, and then

[5] It will be remembered that she met him when her father was ambassador in Vienna.

no sparkle or interest, or talk such as she had been used to hear as a girl. Homeopathy, fresh air, religion, gardening—these were some of her avenues of escape. The little bottles of globules and the little tracts came out of the capacious pockets of her silk aprons. She founded a Society to teach people to sleep with open windows and her bedroom was absolutely honey-combed with devices for letting in fresh air. The people in the cottages she visited rushed to open their windows when the little undaunted figure came into sight.'

Mundell, the head gardener, probably understood her as well as anyone. She spent hours going round the greenhouses with him, the Peach and Nectarine Houses, the Vinery, the Cucumber, Fig and Carnation Houses, the Fern and Mushroom Houses. One echo of Moor Park comes when I re-read *Mansfield Park*, because of the Moor Park apricots to which Mrs Norris was partial, and which were well known even in Sir William Temple's day.

I like to think of my grandfather and his brother Dick, disciples of William Morris, insisting on having the flower beds in the Italian garden filled with sunflowers, which drooping about untidily, were soon replaced by statutory lobelias and geraniums.

The Grosvenor daughters grew up with fluent French and Italian, but very little knowledge of the literature of either country (there were never any books to be seen lying about at Moor Park, only 'sets' behind gilt wire grills). Both could coax a respectable amount of music from the harmonium in the Hall. Driving donkeys in tandem became a craze, and donkeys, their whims and general intractability, dominate the family albums, with photographs of Siss (goddaughter of the Queen's mother, the old Duchess of Kent, whom in girth she resembled) overflowing a small donkey-cart in the main street of Rickmansworth.

Conversations at meals had to be full of jokes to fill the silences, jokes about social *contretemps*, for they loved the grotesque misfortunes of humanity, people swallowing their false teeth at the dinner-table, the curate losing his trousers while wading into a pond to rescue his hat.

Life was an odd mixture of parsimonious and wasteful. I like to think of Char's ancient lady's maid who had been with her since the Embassy days in Vienna, who wore her hair plastered down with a wax preparation called 'bandoline' in a bygone fashion; of the Viennese baker dressed in white duck overalls, baking Viennese *torte* in an oven fed with brush-wood; of the Dairy lined with blue and white Delft tiles with large china cows of Doulton-ware; of the whole unco-ordinated *façon-de-vivre* which no one particularly enjoyed, maintained by a standing army of bored servants. By the older generation of Ebury Grosvenors taken for granted.

As I have said, Robert was fond of small economies. Occasionally there would be an enquiry as to why the household bills were so large, and a family conclave would be called to pool ideas for retrenchment. It would come to nothing. The horses had to be exercised and the stablemen employed, so hunting was obligatory even if it had not been much enjoyed. After-luncheon coffee could be perhaps given up? And the fuel for bedroom fires which led to people lurking in their bedrooms? The house-rule was no bedroom fires from March to October, and the lumps of coal in the bedroom scuttles were strictly numbered (strong opposition to this). One of these conclaves at Moor Park ended with great grandfather Ebury leaving the room, loftily remarking 'we must just do the best we can'. Agreement had been reached that Albertine's canary must be given away because it consumed such prodigious quantities of bird-seed, and that Charlotte should be allowed to indulge her penchant for gloom by having only one oil-lamp to light the White Saloon, where they sat after dinner, so that her daughters-in-law tripped over footstools and mislaid their embroidery silks.

My grandmother having known a London childhood had a sharpened appreciation of country sounds and sights. 'Many delightful memories come back to me of rides through Cassiobury woods,' she wrote, 'of returning tired but very happy in the winter's evening to the stable yard, full of twinkling lights. The clank of a stable bucket, or the hissing of a stableman as he grooms a horse, will always give me a feeling of homesickness. Very pleasant in their way were the long drives in the victoria with Lordship in the afternoon. How well I grew to know the road to Watford, and the various shops where Lordship was a well-known customer. Then there were long quiet drives, mostly in winter afternoons, to Pinner by Ruislip, or along the valley by Mill End to Denham, or up the hill towards Chorley Wood. The steady pace of the horses, the cold air and the warmth of many fur rugs and hot water tins, would induce a very strong inclination to sleep.' How vivid is the picture of the two, fur-muffled, clopping along the unfrequented lanes darkened by overhanging branches, of what was then, but is now no longer, deep country.

The Grosvenor brothers were all splendid skaters and at the first sign of a hard frost they used to have the pond in the Pleasure Ground swept, and flooded by the Rickmansworth fire engine, in order that its surface might be perfect for figure-skating. This was almost the only thing which was ever known to lure Norman from his self-denying ordinance of four hours' piano practice every day. It is an impressive picture—the four tall men, Norman the tallest and the only bearded one, all in tight frogged coats and fur hats, arms folded, executing with absolute concentration complicated figures of eight, glissades, and twirls.

There blew into this claustrophobic routine a fresh wind from the West in the person of an American bride, Tommy Grosvenor's, a Miss Sophia Wells Williams from Boston. How I wish I had known her when she was younger, I can so well see how her American outspokenness must have alarmed the Grosvenors! Her dry comments on all of them are so apt.

Sophie's earliest childhood memory was of hearing newsboys on the quay at Boston shouting the fall of Fort Sumter as the ship in which she and her family were sailing to China,[6] drew away from the side; the first salvo to be fired in the American Civil War. Tommy was a diplomat, and she was to entertain for him at The Hague and in St Petersburg. They always came back to Moor Park for part of the year. She wrote: 'It took a little time to learn all the ins and outs of life in that beloved household. None of them had ever really grown up; they had all (just) grown older doing the things they had always done, in the same way. Music was taboo because Siss liked Handel, Norman something else, and Dick was a Wagnerian to the bitter exclusion of any other composer. Politics were safer left alone. His Lordship was a Whig of the most conservative type; Dick and Algy were Bolshevists, or what seemed so in those days—they were followers of William Morris. Norman had been an ardent Liberal, but, with a breadth of view I always admired, when he saw where Gladstone's leadership was leading,[7]

[6] Her father was a Chinese expert, that is, he both spoke Chinese and knew a great deal about Chinese culture. He was attached to the US Minister's staff in Peking and wrote the (then) standard work on China called *The Middle Kingdom.*
[7] This must have been on the issue of Irish Home Rule.

ceased to follow him. Siss and B were members of the Primrose League, Tommy being a diplomatist had no politics. Religion was never mentioned because the family was divided between High and Low, Agnostic, and nothing in particular. The old man used to fag little Garrett, the parson at Northwood, to come down and give him a Communion service all to himself in his sitting-room at Moor Park, for no reason I could think of except that it annoyed his daughters. If you ever listened to an argument on any of these subjects— music, politics, religion—you realized that if you were not to be torn limb from limb, games were, on the whole, the wisest topic!'

Every August was given over to village cricket, as was happening in every entrenched stronghold in the British Isles, to an accompaniment of vast lunches, stupendous teas, drawing-room theatricals, and amateur concerts in the Village Hall. It was all fairly mysterious to an American: 'Cricket shop was talked until the very word to this day conjures up heated discussions that began at breakfast and ended with bedroom candles, while her Ladyship sat wearily through it all trying hard to seem interested, though to her dying day I do not think she knew the difference between a bowler and a batsman.'[8]

Charlotte Ebury had never expected to have to receive an *American* into the Moor Park circle. She had been largely brought up abroad, in Madrid and Vienna, and believed herself to be without insular prejudice; her uncle Marquis Wellesley had married as his second wife an American widow whom all the family had liked. Yet the word American had distasteful associations. The Civil War had dragged its four-year length like a desperately wounded animal refusing to die, to end with the defeat of the South and all that was mannered and elegant and civilised to British eyes. In his *American Notes* Dickens had praised the city of Boston and its institutions, but given an unfavourable account of Boston ladies. *American Notes* had been published in 1842, had caused a great stir at the time and fixed the British point of view about the New World.[9] Confusedly, the British felt that America was in spirit if not in fact still an English colony. It was permissible only to intermarry with an American if the lady was very

[8] Sarah, Lady Lyttleton exclaimed helplessly: 'It is amazing how all our plans and arrangements are mixed up with *cricket* nowadays—and all the time I understand no more of the subject than an owl!'
[9] See Appendix on Lady Emmeline Stuart Wortley's travels in America.

very rich, which Sophia Wells Williams was not. (It is doubtful if
the elder Grosvenors read Trollope's *The Duke's Children*—
certainly Henry James's *The Bostonians* if it came into the house
at all would have got no further than Caroline's sitting-room. She
and its author became friends years later.)

   That Charlotte had tried her best to prevent the marriage Sophie
knew; it took a long time to break down her mother-in-law's
perfectly polite but distant manner to her, which distressed the
sons who had to a man taken Tommy's wife to their hearts. She
won in the end, being far too intelligent not to appreciate
Charlotte's quality and give her prejudices their due.

   'The welcome I received was past all belief,' she wrote to Susie
(my mother) about three years after Tommy's death, 'from the
kind footman who whispered to me as he met me at the station,
"We are all sorry for you", to your grandfather who gave me a
home. No words can quite describe the kindness, the generosity,
the whole-hearted friendliness of Moor Park. Never for a moment
were you made to feel that you were a stranger. . . .' This, in spite
of small daily battles about who should pour out tea ('Grosvenor
wash'), B. thinking it her prerogative, Sophie quietly assuming the
task as his Lordship had become very fond of her and liked her to
do it. Winters were spent in 35 Park Street, which, though a dark
house, looked out on the gardens of Grosvenor House and the
moving branches of trees that divided it from Hyde Park. Sophie's
affectionate teasing of her in-laws found its way onto paper—I
have on the table before me a manuscript volume of some imaginary 'dialogues' she wrote from which I cannot resist quoting : –

Scene : – 35 Park St., on a very foggy morning after prayers. Big
lamp on breakfast table.

B. (bouncing up from her knees and cornering the Hog)[10]
    Liddiard, don't you think you could find a pair of shaded
    candles to put by my Lord's plate so that the lamp could be
    taken away? My Lady cannot bear the light.

Liddiard   Haven't got a pair.

(B. disappears, toils up to the top of the house and brings down
her little lamp with a dark red shade, which she places by *Ldsp's*
plate).

[10] The cross Moor Park butler, disliked by all of them but for some
reason tolerated.

Sophia (with great asperity) I really do not see the use of making everybody miserable for the sake of an imaginary woe of her Ladyship's. (The Hog takes away the big lamp and the room is left in darkness save for a dim red twinkle by the 1st Baron's plate. Sophia gropes for the toast.)

B. (cheerfully while she feels for her knife and fork) I think the fog is lifting.

Ldsp. (suddenly aware of the gloom) Hello! What's the matter with the lamp? I can't see with this thing—take it away.

B. I put it there, Papa, because Mama cannot bear a lamp at breakfast—it makes her quite ill.
(His Lordship contemplates his plate mournfully while the footman stands patiently tendering him the buttered toast which he cannot or will not see).

Sophia George is offering you the toast, Lordship dear. It will be necessary soon to blow a foghorn when we approach each other, as B. won't let us see anything.

Enter *Ladyship* (who cheers up the minute she sees how dark it is)

Ladyship What a dear little lamp—whose is it?

B. (joyfully) Mine, Mama.

Ldsp I can't see the way to my mouth with this detestable lamp. (pointing to the flame under his cocoa) Shall I put this out? It gives a great deal of light.

Ladyship (to B.) What does he say?

B. Nothing, Mama, that you need pay any attention to.

Ldsp (loudly) I am saying that it is very difficult to see without the big lamp.

Ladyship Oh no!—it is so dreadful to have that glare. Can't you see by that dear little lamp? I'm sure you can if you try.

(Mercifully at this moment the fog lifts).

Charlotte was by the 1880s very frail and her eyes hurt her, which made her seek darkness like a little owl; her deafness was largely assumed to prevent her from hearing what she did not wish to have to take note of. The meals at Moor Park were lavish in the way of cream and butter from the home farms, marvellous peaches, apricots and small pale pineapples from the hot houses, but frugal in the matter of meat, for Charlotte was a food-faddist as well as a homoeopathist and would have liked to banish meat and game from the family dinner table altogether.

Moor Park. Christmas, 1890

Ladyship (as the turkey is handed round) Well, here he is at last, now I hope you will all be satisfied. I'm sure he has been asked for often enough.

Dick What, no sausage? Whoever heard of turkey without sausage?

Ldsp You must not expect too much at once, it has cost her Ladyship a great deal to make up her mind to give us turkey at all.

Sophie The best part of a turkey is having it cold next day.

Caroline Oh, but we must have the legs devilled.

Ladyship Not made into mince? He makes such good mince.

All Oh, dear no—cold—not done up in any way.

B. I must have enough to take to 'mother' tomorrow for her dinner.

(Looks of gloom as it is recollected what a good appetite Mother Gristwood, one of B.'s 'poor women', has).

Ldsp (as he upsets a tumbler of Seltzer water into his lap). Dear, dear, what have I done? (jumps up) By jove, it's gone through, I feel very damp about the legs! Liddiard! Where's Liddiard? I say, get me some dry things. (Footmen rush with napkins) No, no, that won't do, I must have dry things. It's gone right through—get me another waistcoat. What a lot of water one tumbler can hold to be sure! (dabbing vigorously).

Dick[11] (sotto voce) Good reason for not becoming a teetotaller.

Liddiard (arriving with things on his arm) Here's your coat, my Lord.

Ladyship (suddenly waking up to the fact that there is a commotion) What is the matter with his Lordship?

---

[11] The Hon. Richard Grosvenor.

Caroline (to Ldsp) Her Ladyship wants to know what has happened to you.

Ldsp Is anybody speaking to me? (To Liddiard) No, no, the other way, I want my pocket. Where are my glasses? I had them a moment ago. (Shakes each leg) I'm very damp about the legs still. (Reseating himself) Big pardon for making such a disturbance, 'pon my word I was very wet. (Feels his legs again) Just fetch my rug, somebody, from my room, and my small black cap from the pocket of my other coat. (B. hastens away, there being Liddiard, an under-butler, a Groom of the Chambers and two footmen behind the screen to wait on eight people. B. returns, breathless, with the rug and cap). Thankee my dear, now I shall do, I think. (Sneezes).

Sophia (sternly) Lordship, how dare you sneeze when I have not given you permission? Take some coculus.

Ldsp. Well, I would, only the last time I took a globule of it it disagreed with me in the most extraordinary way. Gave me very odd dreams. Mercurius would be the best thing to take, wouldn't it, Ladyship?

Ladyship. (to Norman) What *does* he say?

Norman He wants to know what you would take when you are recovering from drowning.

Ladyship Oh. Bryonis, and then Mercurius.[12]

Ldsp. Very well, I'll take a couple of globules when I go to bed.

(Mince pies arrive and are greeted with much enthusiasm).

Sophia Now Caroline, do your trick.

Hugh[13] (who has not assisted at a Moor Park Christmas before) What's that?

Sophia Caroline always eats fire on these occasions, it's the yearly mark of respect paid to the season. Oh, Liddiard, more brandy than *that*! (as he administers a very small dose to each pie).

---

[12] Homoeopathic remedies with which out of love for Charlotte the whole family allowed itself to be dosed.
[13] Bo's son.

Dick No thank you—not for me. How anyone can eat *hot* mince pie when they can have it cold next day! Caroline, you must have a throat like iron—how *dare* you?

On such an occasion I know that Grandmama (as I was brought up to think of her) would be dressed in black fashioned for long wear, on her head a lace cap with purple ribbons, round her neck a tiny watch with a gold face on a chain set with onyx beads and pearls. As she grew old and diminished in size, her aquiline Wellesley nose became more defined. Grandpapa looked as if he had been cut out of black paper, so thin and tall was he, a high collar cutting his chin off. B., small, plaintive and lame, was overshadowed by Siss (Albertine), enormously fat and tall with it, on the whole a happy woman because of her music and her love of driving and of horses. These she was always vigilant to protect from overwork, which her brothers resented, thinking that it was the opposite of overwork from which the inmates, animal and human, of the Moor Park stables would be likely to suffer.[14]

To me, the 'Uncles' whom I never saw are dim figures and their wives dimmer, excepting always Sophie. She was invariably (I never saw her otherwise) as elegant as a crisp leaf, or a fine kid glove. Not a beauty, though a little like Queen Alexandra, with, when I remember her, the same dry fringe and boned lace collar (but they all sensibly took to these as soon as their necks began to age).

I see in my mind's eye (I only saw it in real life under dust-sheets) the dining-room at Moor Park used occasionally as a ballroom, as my mother (Susie) has often described it to me, a long room running the length of one side of the house, with tall Venetian windows opening three quarters of the way down their length onto a broad balcony. The table was lit by chandeliers; all I saw of them was an imprisoned glimmer through enormous holland bags. Along the great table the family sat, widely spaced out, while the small children of the family deployed their Noah's Ark animals among the garlands and looped ribbons of a Savonnerie carpet.

The table was wide enough for my grandfather to extend his

[14] The sisters after the parents died removed themselves to a house in Cheyne Walk. They did not get on with Bo's wife, Minnie, who entertained smart parties at Moor Park. I just remember being taken to tea with two frail quavery old ladies who treated my mother as if she were my age.

long legs under it without kicking his vis-à-vis. 'Dull Nursery food,' my grandmother once said, 'and never anything out of season.' It was served on green Sèvres china, warmed by being dipped in hot water just before leaving the kitchen, cold before reaching the dining-room, while the conversation went round and round the time of trains from Rickmansworth or Northwood, or the appointment of a new schoolmaster.

Caroline got away after eleven years, during which time Norman was in London for most of the week on business. Feeling that moss was growing over her she made her two daughters' education an excuse for the move. 'It, Moor Park, grew to oppress me with the weight of the tomb,' she wrote, 'and I found myself longing for a life of far less ease but of greater variety and colour.'

Though she loved the country, she was really a Londoner; she and Norman with their daughters Susan and Margaret set up in a small rent-free house in Green Street on the Westminster estate, within easy walking distance of 'the old family' in Park Street. The garden had one sooty fig tree in it; she had a tiny studio of her own at the very top of the house. The little girls had a governess who was a good walker, so they spent a lot of time in museums and art galleries. It was rather cramped but at least it was their own. She was happy, and he, for the first time in his life, content.

The image of my grandfather, set before me by my mother, has been an odd mixture of a sportsman—one who loved to wear old tweeds and caps tufted with fishing flies, yet who was an astute Chairman of the Sun Life Insurance Company, excelling at all games, a composer, a compulsive reader, a traveller—the overall picture, somehow, not adding up to a personality. To be a fine fisherman, a crack shot, an elegant skater and tennis player as well as a businessman, would not be incompatible. The muffling beard, the thick long hair, give him a contemporary look; in his photographs the eyes are gentle, one would think him a person of relaxed temper and infinite benevolence. In fact he was often unhappy to the point of despair, an agnostic, a Radical, a venter of strong unorthodox opinions, a seeker, a born loner.

Years later, long after Norman had died, Caroline was to get a letter from Burne-Jones' widow in answer to one of her own in which she had recalled long ago evenings spent by herself and Norman at The Grange, Fulham (another of London's lost country-houses).

'How well (dear Caroline),' Georgiana Burne-Jones wrote, 'I understand your clinging of heart to those who knew you in your old life. That evening at The Grange when we sat out after dinner in the garden will always remain in my memory and the eager days when Norman and Dick came to lunch every Sunday and drank up Edward's words! Well, what we have truly *had* we can never lose, can we?'

The gentle philosophy of this, so characteristic of the writer, can have been of little comfort to Caroline who missed Norman to the last hour of her life. She described The Grange to me so that I can see it as if the property-developers of today had never laid hands on it. To the child Rudyard Kipling, who spent his holidays there, the knocker on the front door was the summons to Paradise. The leaf-patterned rooms led to the brightness beyond of one of London's hidden gardens, almost an acre of space and secrecy. This door was Norman's entry to Paradise too. I know intuitively what it meant to him to be admitted to an intellectual feast for which he had all this time been starving. Feeling as I do so in sympathy with him, I feel also that this is the moment (with my mother still a child and her marriage to my father two decades away) to take a granddaughter's part in trying to explain him, the rebel in a family of conformers. Removed from him by two generations and two wars I found him in his diaries which had lain in a trunk in an attic of my mother's house for over seventy years, and sitting in a garden all one summer day I was made to feel the eager years.

So strong was Wellesley tradition that Norman went into the Grenadier Guards at the age of twenty, leaving five years later when the family constituency of Chester became vacant and was offered to him. In 1873 Gladstone was offered this Liberal seat which Norman was thankful to vacate. In the end Gladstone did not take it.

Army leaves spent at the Conservatoires abroad confirmed his longing to be a composer, to which end he addressed himself with single-minded concentration in his late twenties, though probably too late for absolute mastery of his art as a pianist. In 'Norman's den', high up under the roof of Moor Park behind the balustrade where 'My Lord', who could not endure 'strummin' ', or Siss, who only tolerated Handel, would not be able to hear him, he worked on harmony and counterpoint, the sounds of his playing like horns of Elfland faintly blowing wove itself into the children's dreams in the night nursery on the floor below.

There are many drawings of my grandfather by his wife, and a delightful one by W. S. Gilbert of him lying full length with a floppy artist's beret pulled over his eyes, titled 'Resurgam'. He was so tall and thin that he found all chairs uncomfortable and was known to stretch himself out on the floor of a railway carriage in order to sleep.

Blanks in his diaries probably belong to the yearly cricket season at Moor Park—cricket being given holy reverence in country-houses, or grouse-shooting in Scotland at which he excelled, throwing himself into games and sport with the same nervous intensity that he put into mastering a difficult passage of piano music. He found meals at Moor Park both heavy and long, the endless discussions about Church matters destructive and depressing.

One entry in the diaries is revealing: 'All my good family have gone to Windsor and have left me sole possessor of a noble mansion and many servants. I rather like the idea of possessing so much, if only for a week.' He was happy wandering in the fields and reading in the garden but a few days of Moor Park living, in the rigid style imposed by old spoilt family servants, were enough. He wrote: 'Very tired; I am always tired now in the mornings, my nights are so restless that it is almost a farce to say that I sleep. I have wandered about, almost driven mad by sad thoughts and the luxuriant beauty of this place. The intense glory of the place oppresses me.'

He had had an unhappy love-affair, strung over some years. His solace was music, but musical perfection eluded him. Yet he was as capable of being uplifted as cast down. After hearing a performance of *Comfort ye, my people*, he wrote: 'Words fail me to describe the power which this music has over me, the acute bodily pleasure and the noble aspirations that I feel. What a true comfort Handel is and what a dolt I must be not to have thought so always.' He speaks of himself as being *haunted unbearably* by certain passages of music, of being in such an agony of delight that he could hardly turn the pages of the score, his hands trembled so.

His real life was lived uncomfortably in London at the top of the dust-sheeted family house, 35 Park Street, ministered to by a caretaker. There he had a piano on which he steadily practised three or four hours a day, working in the evening at political economy, reading Mill and Fawcett, turning over in his mind the perpetual problems of population and poverty, of re-distribution of land, of the relations of Capital and Labour. His politics were mildly Radical which upset his cousin and patron, Westminster. He was out of politics by '74, and much involved with the Monday Pops[15] at which he played, and the foundation of The People's Concert Society for which he was solely responsible; launched four years after Sir Walter Besant's novel appeared containing a Utopian, and, as it turned out, prophetic dream of a People's Palace of Culture in the East End, and two years before Emma Cons acquired the lease of the Old Victoria Music Hall to turn it from a gin-palace into a theatre for the people. In the early days of the People's Concerts admission was by programme costing one penny, the quality of the music depended on the generosity of musicians who gave their services. The running cost came out of the individual pockets of a committee of which Norman was Chairman. The Society threw its net wide, over Barking, Bermondsey, Canning Town, Somers Town, Poplar, Wandsworth, and kept going for fifty-seven years, long after Norman had died and Hubert Parry had succeeded him.

He was beginning to acquire new friends, roaming London on foot with his favourite brother Dick. Their friendship with Burne-Jones led to visits to William Morris at Kelmscott House in Hammersmith.

35 Park Str.

Feb. 15th. Walked round the Serpentine before breakfast, worked all the morning and except for a quarter of an hour's walk after lunch, on again till 5, then went to Miss Octavia Hill's[16] where we rehearsed Mendelssohn's 42nd Psalm for two hours. Went in a storm of rain and snow to dine at The Grange. B-J and his wife were in splendid form, we got onto the immortality of the soul after dinner, they believe in it and in a state of probation to attain the requisite purity. I am revelling in George Meredith's *Evan Harrington*—I hardly dare read on for fear of losing the pleasure.

A letter folded between the pages drops out.

[15] Popular Concerts for the music-loving lower classes.
[16] Co-founder of the National Trust.

The Grange, Northend Road, Fulham S.W. No date

Dear Norman, a wintry & corrupt old heart revives at the sound
of your youthful enthusiasm—, O how young you are, my dear
boy, to like my work and to say so—and how foolish I am to be
pleased and tickled and chirpy at it—for pleased I am, my dear.
Come often and revive me and take in return wise and prudent
counsel which I have always to give—and remain young as I
cannot. Your old N. B-J. (Ned Burne-Jones)

35 Park Street.

Feb. 21st. Walked down to William de Morgan's (workshop)
where I gave way so far as to buy a beautiful plate. I think of
all my friends he is the one who has the most beautiful character,
I doubt if he could do anything wrong if he tried ever so hard;
the only person he ever injures is himself by his almost too
scrupulous sense of honour, which in these days of heavy com-
petition render his anything but a lucrative employment. I don't
think he has ever made a farthing by his work, all he gets goes
in handsome wages to his workmen and improvements in manu-
facture. He has a charming old mother and a bustling sister who
is Secretary to the People's Concert Society. I often pay them a
visit in the evenings at their modest little house (in Cheyne
Row) three doors further down than the workshop.

A link here with myself—on a window sill near me as I write are
the plates that William de Morgan gave my mother as a wedding
present and that are now mine, depicting ladies in flowing robes
wreathed in acanthus leaves and charming babies, playing, under
a glaze of red lustre that changes in different lights to pink and
mauve and silver. My mother remembered him when he had given
up the craft of tile-making, swamped by the commercialism that
he and Morris so dreaded, and was living for half the year in
Florence and the other half at The Vale in the King's Road,
Chelsea, a house so overgrown with creepers that they had to be
groped through before the front door could be found. It is one
of the frivolous uncaring shames of our time (these words are
Angus Wilson's) that houses such as this and The Grange,
Fulham, were torn down without excuse and their foundations left
exposed until a speculative builder perpetrated some shoddy out-
rage on the site.

Norman and Dick set up a bachelor flat in the family house in

E

Park Street—'I did some arranging of my things (de Morgan
plates, pottery from Morris's workshop) our room looks very smart
in its new attire, Morris' paper, etc. After lunch walked to Notting
Hill to see our new People's Concert Society Centre. I find that it
is quite close to Kensal Green cemetery, rather a melancholy neighbourhood. Walked with Dick to Morris's where we remained till
five; no one can say what a happiness it is to know that man. He
is a hero, poet, philosopher, artist, politician, critic and workman
at once, having all the best qualities of each. I think if I lived with
him I could become great—no, nonsense, I shall never be great,
but Morris certainly makes me happy and refreshes me more than
I ever thought could happen from another human being.' Ned was
to write (to Lady Horner) after the death of Morris: 'It was so long
a time, wasn't it?, and meant youth and growth and wonder, and
a world to conquer; and as time goes on we shall see what a world
he conquered. I must confess (his) death makes death more
glorious . . .'

This interest was very timely because Norman had been suffering
one of his recurring fits of pessimism, *jours de cafards* he called
them, cockroaches being the blackest of crawling creatures that he
could imagine. 'Had some conversation with Dick over my affairs,
among other things that I was going to give up the impossible task
of becoming a pianist.' These fits he described as 'Life-weariness,
like a man at a feast who feels a horrible kind of nausea of all
food.' His readiness to be discouraged about his music went far
beyond the petulance of the amateur. He saw himself as a failure
not only as a composer and pianist but in life itself. He would have
considered it unworthy and egotistical to make a fuss about this,
failure to match up to a private ideal he felt should be accepted
sweetly and cheerfully and the pain of it endured in private.

In 1875 he had stayed with the Wortleys as Charlie's musical
friend, in a house at Kirkoswald near Penrith which they had
taken for the summer. Caroline was of the awkward age between
schoolroom and growing up. She was however allowed to walk
and climb with the two young men. She discovered that this tall
bearded stranger, ex-Guards officer, ex-MP for Chester, was not at
all what these labels implied, but was a serious musician whom
Charlie looked up to, a friend of the romantic Pre-Raphaelite
Brotherhood (she herself aspired to be an artist), had read *Middle-
march* with feelings too deep for words and had met the author,

had seen the young Ellen Terry five times as Portia and thought her more magical each time. Caroline spoke good German, and as it was obligatory for musicians to understand German in order to study at Munich, Norman wrung her parents rather reluctant consent to teach their daughter harmony in return for practising his German conversation with her (a maid sitting in the room with them).

The Stuart Wortley parents perceived a foregone conclusion. They had had themselves to endure a long engagement and their love had not moulted a feather. Still Caroline was far too young to be allowed to consider herself engaged, she was not even 'out'. The lessons went too well; his German improved rapidly, her grasp of harmony less rapidly (she was always to prefer being a listener to a performer).

After the winter of '76 the parental foot was put down. They were not to consider themselves engaged or to meet or exchange letters. Caroline had her drawing, he his music. It was the harder on him than on her; he had been so attracted by the easygoingness of the Stuart Wortley family, by its fresh climate of ideas on art, literature, philosophy, expressed and argued forcibly and with heat by five sisters and two brothers. Into this charmed circle he had been welcomed as one of them. It is difficult to see why Norman and Caroline were made to wait so long, but her father's health was deteriorating and her mother could spare little time from his bedside. Margaret's engagement to Reggie Talbot culminated in their marriage in 1880, all the arrangements for it being taken off Jane's shoulders by his sisters, Lady Pembroke and Lady Brownlow. Charlotte, an infrequent letter writer, was moved to write to Caroline at this time:

Moor Park.

My dr. Caroline,

I am not one of many words—therefore I write a *little* line to say how fully I join in all that (your mother) says of sympathy in your trial of long waiting. I know how painful it must be and how you will feel at your sister's marriage the delay of your own hopes. But there is one comfort in that with N's [Norman's] firm character and great affection for you, the delay will increase his appreciation of happiness when it *does* come. It will also make him the more gladly accept any little privations which small incomes must encounter. All that I wd. entreat of you, dear Caroline, for both your sakes, is to (practise) steadfast adherence to your own religious views (in order) to bring him back by degrees to that Faith which he held in early Youth and has so unhappily forsaken. Upon that Faith and that alone (however present care may blind us) depend the real joy and peace of life, and the power of bearing contentedly its inevitable trials—human strength is mere weakness when the day of sorrow comes.

I do deeply deplore his departure from this Faith. But if he sees *you* constant in prayer and finding strength in all the duties of religion—while loving and making him happy—he *may* be won back, and what untold blessing that wd. be to us all. God bless you, dear Child.

Caroline had so attuned her mind to Norman's during their long engagement that adjustment to his ideas was not difficult. I remember her as non-church going and regretful about it. She had been brought up as a believer, but for his sake she was ready to abjure, not that Norman would ever have exacted this.

It is, generally speaking, the mutual friends of a marriage that give it stability. Caroline was ready to worship Morris but found him abrupt and alarming. The weaving and dyeing of stuffs now interested him less, printing on linen had given place to printing books on hand-made paper at the Kelmscott Press, set up in the house in Hammersmith where Norman and Dick had spent so many of the eager days. Kelmscott itself, the low gabled manor in a sea of corn, no longer housed the quick forge that had wrought such enchantment. Morris has enshrined it in his *News from Nowhere*, but the idyll if it ever was a reality, was now over. Caroline shuddered at the cold of it and much preferred to stay with the Charles Booths at Gracedieu, the Carlisles at Nowarth, the Humphrey Wards at Stocks, the Hugh Bells at Rounton. I find it illuminating that Norman's closest men friends were Leslie Stephen[17] and Charles Booth,[18] and that through his friendships

[17] Mountaineer, reformer, philosopher, essayist, the first editor of the *Dictionary of National Biography*, father of Virginia and Vanessa Stephen.
[18] Author of *Life and Labour of the People of London*, to write which he shared working people's lives.

with Edmund Gurney and Frederick Myers[19] he was drawn into their researches into the survival of human personality after death. Both Leslie Stephen and Charles Booth had turned from orthodoxy and the established Church, Booth to give his life up to writing about the condition of the poor, Stephen to relinquish Holy Orders for a career in literary journalism. These three met at London stations to take trains to the nearest countryside, where they would walk and talk the sun down for a whole day, calling themselves the 'Sunday Tramps'. The three, with many other like-minded friends, Frederick Pollock and Douglas Freshfield among them, professed indifference to weather. One of their number set it out in verse:

> Though surely we all by our rule
> Are as peripatetics defined,
>   Yet each philosophical school
> Is here with each other combined,
>   Idealists, realists, find
> Representatives here, as we stalk
>   In the breezes, like them unconfined,
> Over hills of clay, gravel, or chalk . . .

'A new friend sought out Charles Booth at this time (1888–89) and penetrated his smiling reserve, Norman Grosvenor of the Westminster family, a gifted musician who wished to move out of his own aristocratic groove into other worlds. When Norman Grosvenor died Charles said he felt he had lost his only friend. They were both rather isolated men, whose outlook estranged them from their own kin.'[20]

Walter Bagehot, another wistful agnostic, had written earlier: 'There is much of mankind that man can only learn from himself. Behind every man's external life, which he leads in company, there is another which he leads alone, and which he carries with him apart. We all come down to dinner, but each has a room to himself.' At some point in his life Norman must have gently withdrawn himself into this inner room and through his music found the answer to the question of dogma being heatedly discussed but never resolved, round the Moor Park dinner table.

[19] Co-founder of the Society for Psychical Research.
[20] *Victorian Aspirations*, the life of Charles and Mary Booth by Belinda Norman Butler.

Norman's agnosticism was never a piece of intellectual arrogance but grew naturally from his long love affair with music. He was not the first to equate music with the promise of eternal peace. No musician can be unaware of a huge, incomplete pattern that will eventually resolve all questioning in a sublimely satisfying coda.

The composing went on, a *Serenade for Strings* was planned, to be laid aside for nearly all his married life, his settings of songs from *A Child's Garden of Verse*, and his arrangements for several voices of passages from Shakespeare, of the poems of Robert Burns and of Christina Rossetti were sung at Monday Pops by Simms Reeves.

Norman and a cousin, Seymour Egerton, had been some years earlier to the Munich Conservatoire for a winter. Now he made the decision to go there again and have his musical future decided for him. He knew the great Rheinberger, who agreed to take him as a pupil, and went humbly, expecting to be damped; there was however to be no damping, Rheinberger liked his work and did not tell him to throw up composing and go into business, though this in fact was what Norman had been making up his mind to do, for the ban on announcing the engagement had been lifted. Moor Park would absorb Caroline after marriage and any babies, until he was earning enough to support his own establishment; the marriage could take place any day now and did, six months after Jem's death in 1881.

After the Norman Grosvenors had moved into No. 30 Upper Grosvenor Street, the small house in Green Street having become too tight a fit with two growing daughters, there came into their lives a new friend, Walford Davies,[21] who was to do so much for English and Welsh music. Both he and Norman shared a dislike of excessive musical professionalism, and of the kind of snobbery that excluded the talented amateur. Norman wrote to awake and to feed a hunger which he understood, latent, as he believed, in every man whether musically educated or not. He would, he realised, never now be a performer of the highest rank. Always diffident about his own talents, he turned for truthful assessment to Walford Davies, kindliest of critics, who wrote after his death

---

[21] Sir Henry Walford Davies, a musical scholar, organist of St George's Chapel, Windsor, Master of the King's Musick, composer of *Solemn Melody* for organ and strings, '*God be in my Head and in my Understanding*' and much else.

about his friend's unfinished *Serenade for Strings*: 'He completed three movements, and he left sketches for a fourth and last. This final movement was to have been a lighthearted Rondo: and I remember, with pleasure and regret, how on an evening not very long before his death he played a charming Haydnesque theme of some twelve or sixteen bars, only to look up with his usual diffidence, anxious for a second opinion, with a look that plainly said, "This won't do, will it?" '

After seventeen happy years of marriage to Caroline, Norman died of inoperable cancer. The darkened house with straw laid down in the street to muffle the noise of horse-drawn cabs and carts, deeply scarred his children's memories. Susie, my mother, wrote many years later: 'When my father died, my sister and myself were sent to sleep in old Grosvenor House (next door) accompanied by a maid, for the family was away and the rooms on the ground floor were dust-sheeted and ghostly. I remember my despairing misery when I woke in the morning. The ceiling of the bedroom was covered with stout cupids who disported themselves on unreal clouds against an azure sky, they wavered and dissolved before my tear-dimmed eyes.'

Norman lay in a room filled with flowers sent up from Moor Park. When the end was mercifully near, a friend played her violin softly outside his door. In delirium he had played on the sheet as on his piano, endlessly, but now the restlessness was stilled. '*Music*,' he said, smiling faintly as he drifted out on the tide. 'Beauty is one of the last toys we have to play with.'

Seven years earlier, Charlotte had slipped out of life, desiring only to give no one any inconvenience by her dying. Mary Lovelace wrote to her sister-in-law, Lady Anne Blunt: 'Lady Ebury is dying. She has been just like a real mother to Caroline, so sweet and kind always to us all. The dreadful thing is that she suffers so much, it is something internal. Her one idea is to assure her poor old husband that it is not as bad as it looks, and that she is quite happy and not at all afraid. Only very good people can die like that . . .'

The winter's day of her funeral at Northwood in the church which she and Robert had built was too cold for the old man. When the mourners returned to Moor Park he told them that he had been having a very nice time, reading the Burial service to his sister-in-law Lily and the kitchenmaid.

8

All the Daughters of my Father's House

My mother, Susan Charlotte Grosvenor, elder daughter of Norman and Caroline, was tall and graceful and wore her long silvery fair hair in a charming swept-up style with a 'tea-pot handle' on top. To watch her brushing it in long sweeps made me as a child confuse her with Rapunzel of the long gold hair in Grimm's fairy story. She could not so much as boil an egg—in a houseful of servants there was no need for her to learn this slight skill—or sew a button on since she had a maid to do it, and had never in her life bought a railway ticket or travelled alone. On her first visit to the Bank House in Peebles to visit her future in-laws, she was amazed at the strenuous housewifery that made life a penance of cold ham and junket during the rites of cleaning that took place every Spring.

She had been patchily taught by a governess chosen for her moral character but for nothing else. Susan and her sister were not conformers. Marnie inherited the musical gifts of her father and wanted only to be a singer—which she became. Susan was bent on improving her mind by gulping down books on religion and philosophy, the longer and duller the better. In this way she read Bergson, Schopenhauer, William James, Amiel's *Journals*, Von Hügel, and learnt pages of German and French poetry (a love of the last she passed on to me). Her aunts approved—girls should have an intellectual interest providing they did not bore their dancing partners with it—the chief aim of their lives being, of course, marriage. Though when Susan became engaged to an Irish *parti* they gave only qualified approval (Irish peers not being quite in the same class as English ones). When she broke the engagement off in order to marry an unknown Scottish barrister called John Buchan, the son of a Presbyterian minister, who was a partner in a (then) unheard of publishing house (dangerously near to being 'in trade'), but who was already being noticed as a writer, they relinquished the principles of an entrenched society and took him to their hearts.

Susan's struggles with Hegel in German and Plato in translation touched my father. He was, as many seemingly confident young men are, in need of someone to teach, and she was teachable and longing to be taught. William de Morgan, a family friend, wanted her to design tiles for him as she had a pretty gift for design, but it was not enough for her. She had inherited the same need for self-improvement that made her father, Norman, seek the friendship of William Morris and Charles Booth.

It is not often possible to say with conviction that two people are made for each other; my parents were. They were married at St George's, Hanover Square, whose Registers contain notices of the marriages of so many of my forebears. As Norman was dead, Caroline gave her daughter away. They drove to the church in the high-sprung Westminster family coach, which made Susan feel queasy. The tightly unsmiling faces of the bridegroom's Presbyterian relations must have provided an interesting contrast to the rest of the fashionable gathering overflowing the pews with frills and hugely feathered hats.

I was born of this happy marriage, the eldest of four, with three brothers—all wanted, encouraged, praised. Before 1914 my parents bought the end of the lease of a large Adam house in Portland Place, destroyed by a bomb in the Second World War. A friend, Hugh Lane the art critic, chose a blue wallpaper for the drawing-room as near as possible to the blue of Robert Adam's original. There were empty niches on the curving staircase for statues. I maintain that from our nursery window I saw a fire-engine drawn by horses, manes flying, nostrils smoking, brass bells clanging, dashing down Portland Place—if so it must have been the very last one in use. What I did see every autumn and winter evening was the lamp-lighter stringing behind him a wavering chain of sparks, and heard the muffin-man's bell. Punch and Judy sometimes came to the street, but was too frightening for us—how could that robust survival of the Commedia dell' Arte ever have been thought suitable for children's entertainment?

Every day in Spring and Summer we walked—that is, I walked by the pram in which my next brother but one rode. There were only two walks, one to the Crescent Gardens to which we had, as residents, a key, or down Portland Place to Regent Street. Looking through a book of Muirhead Bone's etchings of London streets of this date I find a delicate dry-point of Portland Place down which

E*

I watched the lamp-lighter go every evening. There is a child's figure in the etching that might be mine passing the tall iron gates of Lord D'Abernon's mansion—now crushed and obliterated by Broadcasting House, a mansion loved by us because of a grey parrot that sat in a window. In the Portland Place Gardens daisies were free for the picking. The tight bunches tied with grass stalks smelt warm and friendly like home-made cakes. Fallen chestnut-flower heads that did not lend themselves to bunching lay thickly like a pink carpet under the trees; as good as the bluebell carpet in Spring on the floors of the beech woods at Medmenham, where we were sometimes sent to stay with our Talbot great-aunt and uncle. This I remember as happiness, but not unalloyed.

On our way to the Gardens we had to cross the street where a boy crossing-sweeper attempted to sweep up the straw and dung of passing cabs. The motor-car had not yet driven them off the streets. In all the family houses in which we stayed the schoolrooms would have shelves of improving tales published by the Society for the Promotion of Christian Knowledge, stories in which poor children died of lung diseases (brought on by exposure) with woodcuts of heartrending realism. The pang that the crossing-sweeper's torn coat and broken boots cost me I can still recall. I would lie awake on windy nights wondering where that poor boy slept, on what draughty doorstep, for I could only picture him homeless. I begged for pennies to give him till my elders, refusing to hand out any more, gave me careful explanations about the unwisdom of something called 'indiscriminate charity'. There were all degrees of beggars then, no streets were immune from them. The only one we were allowed to give a penny to was an old man with a tremendous beard outside Vere Street Post Office who sold groundsel for canaries, the reason given being that he must have had to go such a long way to pick it and have so few customers for it.

It was, as I now see, the wretchedness of the street-poor of London—crossing-sweepers, cab-runners, match and boot-lace sellers—that started my furious, childish dialogue with God: 'Why, why, WHY, is this sort of thing allowed?' De Quincey wrote of the homeless crouching 'under porches' in Oxford Street, where he picked up the little street-walker whom he befriended and lost. When I came to read Dickens I saw how thin had always been the comfortable layer over the misery, and vowed to dedicate myself to the poor, inexplicably disowned by a Heavenly Father who, I had been taught, was the source of all loving kindness. But I was not gloomy all the time, though we had a rough nurse who disliked my second brother and myself and was the sort who believed in shutting children in dark cupboards and banging them with stiff hair-brushes. However, children are wonderfully resilient and we were no exception.

Ours was, understandably, a bookish upbringing. I loved Scott, Bulwer Lytton, and Stevenson, because they did not write down to children as Kipling, Barrie and Kenneth Grahame subtly did (with a wink to the grown-up reader). *Peter Pan* I secretly thought too silly to be frightening.

I think it must have been after we left London for Oxfordshire, during one Christmas holidays, that I was taken to see a play called *Broomsticks*, written by Walter de la Mare with a star part for Ellen Terry. My elders talked of this actress in tones of reminiscent adoration. What I saw was a dear old granny-person who had to be helped across the stage because she was going blind. She could no longer memorise a part, and lost her place several times in the prompt copy from which she read it, until she dropped the shawls in which she was muffled and opening her arms to include us all, begged us in a voice of warm honey to bear with her. Bear with her! I clapped until my hands were sore, I would have died for her. The theatre was to be my goal. The seed was sown that germinated all through my teens.

I was fortunate indeed in having an aunt who if she had not been the daughter of a Free Kirk minister, could have become an actress in 'pawky' Scotch parts, as her friend Jean Cadell was. She it was who fostered my love of the theatre. This seems as good a place as any to speak of this dearly-loved aunt from Scotland, my father's spinster sister Anna Buchan.[1] As a child I would shut my eyes at the sound of a blind man's stick tapping along the kerb, sick at my helplessness to relieve the world's misery. I do not think a tramp—and tramps were legion in my childhood—ever came to my aunt's door but he had food pressed on him and money for a night's lodging. Indiscriminate charity—blessed be your name!

The word 'spinster' I never understood until in *Twelfth Night* I came on the lines about 'the spinners and the knitters in the sun, and the free maids that weave their thread with bones'. Anna could

---

[1] She wrote delightful stories of life in and around a small town in the Borders called *Priorsford*, under the name of O. Douglas.

never have spun, was no knitter and was far too impatient to master the art of lace-making with ivory bobbins (bones), but a 'free maid' she was to the end and gloried in her state.

She indulged me during her occasional visits to London with intemperate play-going: 'Oh, call back yesterday, bid time return', and let me be for a moment a child again, sitting beside that dear aunt at Wyndham's or His Majesty's, watching the footlights go up and the curtains tremble in the yellow glow! My parents were interested in the theatre though not so besotted, and took me, aged eleven, to see Duse in *Ghosts* (she again was old, and the play in Italian, so not much got through to me; still, I am able to say that I have seen Duse).

After 1918 my father removed us to the country; the contrast between his robust country upbringing and our London existence of pottering walks to the Portland Place Gardens hit him suddenly on meeting us dawdling home with our hoops, white and tired on a baking summer day. He chose the proximity of Oxford where he had been an undergraduate in the nineties at Brasenose—'like some comfortable latter-day monastery', still warmed by the fading sunset of Walter Pater.

The house we had lived in in London had borne the signature of an architect of genius. Elsfield Manor (it was no one's idea of a *manor*), though in the cellars it was twelfth century, in two rooms seventeenth century, had been heightened and enlarged in the 1870s without either imagination or common sense; in a cavernous and almost pitch dark basement the cook had her being and the butler slept (the cook had to take her bad legs up three break-neck flights to *her* bed). We thought it a beautiful house, which it was not, and the garden a Paradise, which it was. Like the children in E. Nesbit's books we dodged and plotted and hid, assuming the characteristics of favourite heroes and heroines (it seems always to have been early morning with white dew powdering the summer lawn or five o'clock of a winter evening after tea and before bed-time), till my brothers at three year intervals went to the Dragon School in Bardwell Road in Oxford and the daughters of my mother's friends came to do lessons with me.

It was to be Art for me, not Music for which I might have shown more aptitude, and I was sent once a week to the Ruskin School of Drawing in the Ashmolean Museum. Ruskin, as I now know, was the most powerful single influence in art and architecture of the last hundred and fifty years. Terraces of artisans' dwellings had their Venetian windows (or a Victorian speculative builder's idea of what Venetian windows should look like) supported by stubby pillars crowned with foliated capitals. Indeed the architecture of Venice on first acquaintance can seem an unnerving duplication of South Kensington. Ruskin's ideas ruled in Art Schools. As I sat on my camp stool in the basement of the Museum, shading industriously with a single-B Venus pencil, I did not, of course, know that Ingres, intent on purging Art of what was meretricious in it, had proclaimed *'surtout le dessin, le dessin est la probité de l'art'* and that the Ruskin school had been founded on this precept. After months of this lonely toil I was promoted to a life-class which took place in an attic in Cornmarket above a hairdresser's. A draped model was permitted to pose for the Ruskin students in the Ashmolean, but a University statute disallowed total nudity other than in metal or plaster, within its walls. (The embargo has now been removed.) Vera Lane-Poole, who had been a pupil of Sickert's taught the life-class with Sydney Carline. It was warmed by a Tortoise Stove so that the half of the model was pink, the rest of her blue with cold. What the visiting teachers thought of the class's absence of talent they were kind enough to dissemble. Their names, Gilbert Spencer, Paul Nash, Albert Rutherston, meant nothing to me then, though deeply venerated by me now.

Elsfield was within walking distance of Oxford, as Dr Johnson found, and it attracted young men drawn there by the *bienséance ordinaire* that was the rule of the house. Susan had no desire to mother young men. In her detached way she poured out tea for them, forgetting to renew the hot water in the pot, too interested in learning about their antecedents (many were the sons and nephews of friends) to offer them cake. Those, and they were legion, who became Sunday-tea habitués, fetched the hot water for themselves and pressed food on latecomers.

The front door of the Manor was on the village street under a porch roofed with Cotswold tiles, and no one would have dreamed of entering without first ringing the front door bell. Some may have found it intimidating to be formally announced, and to venture round the bookcase just inside the library door to confront a roomful of people, lit by the westering sun across forty miles of Oxfordshire. Daunting perhaps on first impact, but not for long.

Those who, toward the end of their university years, had come to look on Elsfield as an extension of home, would go to the bookshelves and take out a book which had attracted them on a previous visit, or go for a turn down the mossy paths that led to all that remained of Francis Wise's water garden;[2] a path from there brought you round by one of those delectable *jardins potagers* where feathery asparagus beds co-existed with peonies, and potatoes with unfashionable roses that seem to have something of the characteristic of the women they were named for—Madame Alfred Carrière, Angele Pernet, Zéphyrine Drouin.

It was said that would-be poets went to Garsington, commencing writers and politicians to Elsfield. Some, not feeling gifted to be writers but beglamoured of the literary scene, wanted introductions to the publishing world; more have made an impact on politics. At weekends there would be practically always a Personage staying who would drop a word in the right quarter, these were the days of indirect personal influence rather than the Corridors of Power.

As I have indicated, I started life in blinkers, in an ordered world, but not one immune from pain and fear. Over my very early years the 1914 war spread like a stain though I cannot have been aware of this at the time; the next war blotted out five years of our lives, so that I, for one, feel as if I had lived through three unrelated eras. When I was beginning to grow up, emancipated girls of the half-generation before me moved into bedsitters on allowances from their parents, and filled them with black and orange cushions and Pierrot dolls. Cigarette holders got longer and longer, and skirts climbed higher and higher. I was without desire to emulate them. They were out to win another war, for a new kind of freedom. I was too young for that, but, desperately unsure of myself, I longed to be in some sort of swim, near to an (imagined) centre.

In the summer—the Elsfield library was an autumn and winter room—we sat in the drawing-room that had survived from Mr Wise's house, white panelled, cool in the evenings. These *recherches* will inevitably be in a wrong sequence, since Mnemo-

[2] Bodley's Librarian who lived at Elsfield in Dr Johnson's day. In his time there had been a cascade, an Egyptian pyramid and a Chinese temple with bells.

syne, mother of the Muses and Goddess of Memory, is too often
the mother of Invention as well and therefore not to be regarded
in the light of a prop. She withholds her gifts of remembering
when most one needs them, to pour out a whole cornucopia at an
unexpected moment. I see one of these in the Elsfield drawing-
room whose windows looked down through a domesticated wood
to a dark pond with a lop-sided temple, all that was left of Mr
Wise's extravaganzas, and there, not diminished by time but the
size they were in life, are three women, Virginia Woolf, Rosamond
Lehmann, Elizabeth Bowen—all dressed for the evening in mothy
shades of brown and grey with some gleams of silver like three of
the Muses, only all three were the handmaids of one Muse, the
divine Thalia, who is always standing in the shadow of her dark
sister Melpomene.

There had been a dinner party and the ladies had retired to the
drawing-room to look at the sunset, Virginia remarking rather
cruelly 'Alice will tell us what it feels like to be eighteen and looking at a sunset'. She was staying in the house. I had the room next
to her and knew she had not gone to sleep early but had stood for
a long time at the window, sighing gustily, then moved about the
room, which was a large one, bumping into things like a moth in
a lampshade, pulling off her rings, letting them fall with a tinkling
crash on the glass-topped dressing-table, all the while talking
rather loudly to herself.

Rosamond Lehmann and Elizabeth Bowen arrived together; in
their dappled chiffons I thought they looked like silver birch trees.
My mother had known Virginia since their girlhood, their parents
having been friends. Elizabeth was an Oxford neighbour. She and
my mother developed a great affection for each other, each
dedicated a book to the other. I was in my late teens when she came
first into my life to remain intermittently in it till the day she drove
away from Charlecote in 1971—where she had enchanted my son's
artist friends while reviving my old fondness for her, calling
back: 'You must go on writing, Alice, promise me you will'—to
go out of all our lives forever a year later.

The country round Elsfield had not changed since the eighteenth
century, the view from the top of the hill that drops down to Old
Marston and Oxford presented, rising from a green muffle of
trees, the historic line of spires and towers and the bubble dome

of the Radcliffe Camera. I suppose I saw this view every day when out on my pony or walking down to classes in Oxford (a mere four miles). My father liked to ride at weekends, he had an old hunter called Alan Breck and I was called upon as a companion which I anxiously strove to be, urging my fat pony to keep up with Alan Breck's long stride. He would rein in at the crest of Elsfield hill and recite the verse from *Thyrsis* which contains the line about the Fyfield elm, then still conspicuous on the Berkshire skyline. I knew the whole poem by heart and listened obligingly, the bored stable-wise horses snatching at their bits. If I had any merit as a companion it was because I had a good memory and was generally a jump ahead of him when it came to quoting.

At the top of Elsfield village to which the road mounted steadily was a farm, and from it the land dropped dramatically. Like Caroline Wharncliffe who, when she was asked to admire the prospect from Wharncliffe Crags, put the Alps out of her mind and declared she had never seen a finer, so happily do I abjure all other views in favour of that of Otmoor, blue as a landscape under the sea, seemingly illimitable.

There my father and I rode for the intoxication of galloping across fields divided only by shallow ditches where in winter flood-water threaded the grassy undulations that were once called 'balks'. I have derived from him an awe of woods. He told me of the 'dancing floors' that were clearings in the old forests, sacred places. He wrote of one of these not far from Elsfield: 'I seemed to be crossing the borders of a Temenos, a place enchanted and consecrate . . .'

I would not have gone to Otmoor alone, even for the marsh pippits' nests or the legendary lizard orchis or the rose-red water-avens. There was an ill omened *something* called locally the 'Moor Evil', perhaps a swamp fever; I saw it as a sort of black miasma rising from the ground to come creeping after me with dreadful stealth. In me an easily inflamed imagination had fed on the ghost stories of Dr M. R. James. I knew that if the Moor Evil was after me I would not be able to outride it.

Between classes in Oxford I wandered through College Quads, in a dream sequence that was part *Zuleika Dobson* part *Sinister Street,* absorbing them. There would be tea in Fuller's shop in Cornmarket or in the steamy Cadena Cafe before the walk home through seedy St Clements up to Elsfield on its hill, none of it built up then; all the way the hedges were thick with scrub elder, the ditches high with Fool's Parsley.

Oxford: the name is so emotive, so charged with thoughts and delights of youth that I feel unequal to writing about it. Then there was the other Oxford, one's humorous country town; deplored for the humdrumness of its shops, to which one went for the dentist and elocution lessons from Rosina Philippi (retired and living in Bardwell Road);[3] a place seen in later life to have become second-rate, not amusing any more.

The people of Elsfield and the household at the Manor kept to the old trodden ways. My youngest brother went to a day-school in Oxford in a pony trap, and village people, who had business in Oxford, bicycled or walked the four miles, or went by the twice-weekly carrier's cart. Having to call at practically every house on the way, the carrier took a very long time, but in those days there *was* more time. Returning after a matineé or a lecture in the early winter dusk one would be comfortably accommodated at the back of the big covered cart among farm implements and live-stock in baskets, and grow sleepy in the warm dark smelling of hessian and straw, with the cart's lantern, like a domestic Will-o'-the-Wisp, sending its shifting circle of weak light now up on the bank, now down on the road.

Elsfield to us was just somewhere to live, a shell within which we expanded at our own pace, grown-up life went on at one level, ours at another, and this was the special grace conferred on children by large households. Our parents' life and ours hardly impinged.

Like all enlightened late Victorians my father felt he had a duty to set an optimistic view of life before the young. When he found me reading Spengler's *Decline of the West* he was really angry, he thought pessimism was the sin against the Holy Ghost. Yet I wonder if he, a classical scholar, really believed this, since the heroic ideal does not exclude an heroic pessimism. When his autobiography came to be written—it was oddly titled *Memory-hold-the-door*—I felt that it should have had as an alternative title the old sundial tag, *'non nisi numero horas serenas'*,[4] so much did it

---

[3] An Italian actress greatly admired in her day, a dynamic teacher who would pound on the piano to force us to shout above the noise. Denne Gilkes, a teacher of singing, who came later into my life was such another. I send those two women my life-long gratitude.

[4] 'I only tell the sunny hours'.

seem to have been written about someone else, not the father I knew who was always ailing from a chronic internal condition and who pushed himself to the limit, and beyond, of his strength.

He had the enviable knack of remembering in detail the sunny hours, and none of the Calvinist's distrust of them. I thought in an unreasoned way that his evident enjoyment of weekends at Cliveden and *intime* dinners at Londonderry House was unworthy of him. I was too young to see that they were to him Disraelian and relished for that reason, and that he perceived the absurdity of snobbery as acutely as Thackeray did. A stony young Puritan, I thought he should have been more selective about the company he kept.[5] I see now that where my father was liked he liked in return, wholeheartedly, and took boyish delight in the trappings of other lives so different to the life he had been born to. He was in the French phrase *'sur son assiette'*; I was no help to him sitting through dinner parties looking so thunderously glum that my grandmother Caroline was moved to remark to my mother: 'That child will never marry while John does all the talking and monopolises the young men who ought to be talking to *her*.'

I have not so far mentioned my father's mother whose brothers were sheep farmers in Peeblesshire and owned a Border farm which was a dearly loved holiday home to us. She was a daughter and widow of the old Free Church of Scotland. A Bible-searcher which, as everyone who has tried it knows, is a rewarding occupation, there being a cominatory phrase in it for every permutation of human frailty. She made my father's life a bed of nails with her daily letters (to which she expected a punctual reply), written at high speed so that her always difficult spiky writing ran into an undecipherable tangle like barbed wire.

And barbed her comments were! She never tired of pointing out to him the danger we were exposed to by being taken to the village church at Elsfield (which was so Low Church that it could not have been Lower). Instinctively understanding my father better

---

[5] Once at a party at Londonderry House, where the footmen were got up in kilts and lace ruffles, and our hostess wore the jewels of an Empress, the Irish writer Sean O'Casey arrived in shabby gray flannels. Londonderry House liked to be thought of as a den of literary lions. O'Casey was not a lion of the first rank. I liked the way he looked amused, not specially impressed.

than she did (to her he had remained and always would remain a clever schoolboy who had gone to England to seek a fortune), I saw how her references to bowing down in the House of Rimmon depressed him. His loyalty to the Church of his fathers, which he possibly felt he had betrayed by marrying into the English aristocracy and settling for a life in England, had to be balanced with the career he had chosen, or had had thrust upon him. He soothed her as best he could, changing the subject by telling her of the brilliant *mots* of the clever people he had been meeting, which far from soothing simply produced another screed. For years I visualised the House of Rimmon as looking like one of the late Victorian villas of North Oxford. I am not much wiser now.

I think that, with the chivalry children show toward their elders, we tried honestly not to make things harder for him by provoking Gran with exhibitions of excessive Englishness. Besides, we were fond of her. Children are governed by their appetites and she was an exquisite baker of scones so light that you could eat a dozen at a sitting and not feel full, she would let us have the 'skimmings' when she made jam, her idea of a 'piece' for a day on the hills was slices of rich black 'bun' spread thickly with butter, and tiny mutton pies kept hot in a napkin. Her hospitality was deservedly famous. 'Never quarrel with abundance,' she once said sternly to me when I, trying to diet, shuddered delicately at a crowded tea-table. She had known what it was to live in genteel poverty as the wife of a Presbyterian Minister who was a scholar and a poet but so hopeless about money that she had to put his exact bus fare in his pocket for him when he went visiting his flock. More often than not he would give it to the first beggar he met and walk home in shoes that let in water.

A tiny dynamo, in the dusty black of a Minister's widow (she went into perpetual mourning when he died), she was welcomed wherever she went. Once visiting with her a Glasgow tenement, where two old ladies of my grandfather's congregation were living in great poverty, I flinched from one of them whose face was horribly disfigured with some corroding disease—could it have been lupus? Gran saw my disgusted expression and determined to teach me a lesson; as we left she drew the poor face down to hers and kissed it.

When she was no longer there, irritating as a piece of grit in the eye, I felt sad and ashamed for, never having been called upon to bring up a large family on a minister's pittance (and with the high Roman courage she displayed). I was a lesser creature in every way.

Though she announced that she only wanted her children's and grandchildren's happiness, she only wanted it on her own terms. She had lost two children, my father had been absorbed into a world she distrusted, the remaining two showed no signs of leaving her, yet she was worldly enough to be impatient of their clinging to her apron strings.

The Old Bank House at Peebles, where she lived in her widow-hood, is being 'planned' out of existence, so that for me the iron gate on to the street has creaked hospitably for the last time. It was a kindly house, for there Gran had it all her own way, there she could relax and be tartly amusing, she could even be wryly self-critical. If she had been no relation she would have been my friend, I could have loved her. This is how I *want* to remember her, thinking of those lines of Dr Johnson's about his friend Levet:

> His virtues walked their narrow round
> Nor made a pause nor left a void,
> And sure the Eternal Master found
> His single talent well employed.

But it would be an over-simplification and not fair to her, she was more complicated than that, and finer. I rather choose the good Doctor's valediction on a poor blind lady he befriended: 'She left her little substance to a Charity School. She is, I hope, where there is neither darkness, nor want, nor sorrow.'

There was one autumn and winter in my early teens when my parents went abroad in search of a cure for my father's duodenal trouble, (my brothers were at boarding school) and I was sent up to London to stay with my grandmother Caroline Grosvenor. Old Grosvenor House and its contiguous houses were gone, as I have told elsewhere, and she was living in a narrow tall house, No. 2, in the same street but nearer to the Square. Indoctrinated young, I was at heart a Londoner, and by now fathoms deep in Dickens. If there was a fog I blissfully swallowed the scorching stuff, seeing—as he did—lit shop windows through it like ruddy smears on the brown air. It was thought that I ought to improve my knowledge of painting by visiting galleries, to which end I was provided with pocket money, and many happy hours I passed in the old National Portrait Gallery where the portraits were the colour of soup, learning how the English face changes with the centuries. My grandmother only wanted to spend all her day in her studio, so no difficulties were made though she had her own prohibitions, not quite those which had ruled her sister Mary's art-student days but odd enough. Bond Street must only be walked down in daylight, *wearing gloves*, the Burlington Arcade shunned altogether. There could be no objection to my shopping at the Army and Navy Stores, of which Cousin Francis Ebury was Chairman, provided that I did not cross Hyde Park Corner (but how to get there?). Generally speaking, Victoria was respectable, Kensington dowdy but safe, Chelsea a slum. It would not have crossed her mind to include the City, and anything north of Piccadilly was of course out of the question, since for all one knew Jack the Ripper still prowled there. From her now limited household no one could be spared to accompany me, so I was to be trusted. Regrettable to admit, the moment I was well out of sight of Upper Grosvenor Street I took a bus to the City, prepared with a story about studying the Book of the Dead in the British Museum—which would have interested her, she knew Egypt and had been a friend of Howard Carter, who opened the tomb of Tutankhamen.

By now I was not so squeamish. The run of my father's library had steadied me, the raging pity I had felt as a child was only an ache. The blood-stained post gnawed in his dying agony by the baited bear, the starved children's bodies found by their father hanged in a closet with the note, 'done because we are too menny'[6] —these and many other images of cruelty and injustice, still throbbed, but less. I had gained some idea of the root causes of vagrancy and learnt to rein my frantic imagination.

The City between the wars was still in some ways, and especially in a pea-soup fog, the London of the illustrations of Cruikshank and Gustave Doré. A plain schoolgirl in a mackintosh who had to screw up short-sighted eyes in order to read the names of the streets, I wandered unnoticed in and out of its alleys and courts. Is it still there, Bleeding Heart Yard, where Keats lodged? There were still many dim eating houses with sanded floors where Dick

[6] Thomas Hardy, *Jude the Obscure*.

Swiveller could have lounged at the counter, calling for a pint of
the 'rosy'. My brother William remembers, while staying as a
small boy at the Deanery of St Paul's, eating in a shilling 'ordinary'
for City clerks which had narrow wooden stalls in which Scrooge
could have taken his frugal supper. I had sometimes gone with my
father (but this was many years earlier), to Nelson's publishing
house, of which he was a senior partner, in Amen Court, part of
a warren of ecclesiastically-named alleys round the Cathedral now
obliterated, and being told to amuse myself quietly would sit at a
window entranced by the huge dull silver dome of St Paul's that
seemed to be floating among the clouds.

City churches, their interiors darkened by Victorian ecclesiology,
had the smell of soap and polish of an old-fashioned rectory. One
day in the week, I think Monday, it was possible to go round the
Royal Tombs and Henry VII's Chapel in Westminster Abbey
without paying. My grandmother knew that the British Museum
was free and would have smelt a rat if I had asked for more money
over and above my bus fares, so Monday was my day for the
Abbey, to which she would hardly have objected.

I would take it slowly, savouring the pleasure as Charles Lamb
did, starting with the Cloisters and working round the Statesmen,
treading on my idols, Dickens and Handel (but not yet Byron).
The fanvaulting wheeled above my head till, tranced, I lost all
sense of the here-and-now, and had to sit down in a pew until my
head stopped spinning. I had not then read Morris's *Dream of
John Ball*, but without being told imagined for myself the mason
setting his chisel to the stone—'The chancel was so new that the
dust of the stone lay white on the midsummer grass beneath the
carving of the windows.' I have told of my father's before-bedtime
reading aloud. An occasional choice of his would be a passage from
Morris's verse translations of the Icelandic Sagas or his *Wood at
the World's End* or the *Defence of Guinevere*, to which his slightly
sing-song delivery, with the Border accent that came back to him
when something touched him deeply, was perfectly suited. I would
listen drowsily, realising that in Morris's poetry, as with Shakespeare, I had tapped a fount of words from which I would be able
endlessly to drink.

In the small front drawing-room of No. 2 Upper Grosvenor
Street in a glass-fronted bookcase was the black-letter Kelmscott
Chaucer, given to Norman by Morris; I knew about Kelmscott, I

had been taken there to have tea with Morris's daughter May, an intimidating figure—'tea' being dry seed-cake eaten on a curved high-backed settle. There was a spread of tapestry in an upper room hanging from rusty nails, this much I remembered (a child reared on Scott would notice that), and the old roses which Morris first saw as 'rolling in superabundance' made a green dusk in the rooms. Sitting on the floor of that London drawing-room with the Chaucer in my lap, I pestered my grandmother about Jane Morris, who seemed to me the perfection of beauty. 'She was much admired,' Caroline said without enthusiasm, tugging wool through her tapestry birds. 'Beautiful surely?' 'In her own way. Unhealthy looking. She was a very simple person,' (Caroline meant by this that she was lower-class) 'and didn't care for poetry—or not *his* poetry. He could be frightfully long-winded.' She was not interested, she liked to move on and let the Past take care of itself. I was not going to get any *recherches* out of her.

It was not until many years later that I was to discover more about William Morris. I loved him for trying to create a brave, self-respecting world in an England darkened by the spread of industry. His love, which I share, of field flowers—trefoil and pimpernel, woundwort and eyebright, bramble and woodbine (names as old as Chaucer)—lives in his designs and though much vulgarised still distills a dew from vanished Kelmscott hedgerows. 'Above all, he dignified the craft of letters by a character perhaps the most generous, simple, manly, and dutiful since Sir Walter Scott.'[7] High in my personal Heaven I set this passionate, lonely, humble man who never condescended or gave quarter to faulty work.

My elders, made nervous by all this, suddenly out of a clear sky announced that I was to be sent to a teaching establishment in a suburb of Paris called Vieux Colombes. It was too small to be exactly a 'finishing school', yet that, in the best sense, was what it was. It was a cooling-off period in my case. The fatalism tempered with cool reason that my teachers showed, so characteristically French, worked on my childish resentments and super-heated imagination. It was hoped that I would come down to earth and learn some skills on an unprofessional level, as how to cut out a dress from a paper pattern, how to make a pudding, and so on. I

[7] John Buchan, *Homilies and Recreations*.

and my girl friends and cousins were at an unfortunate age, either too opinionated or too strangled with shyness to be what my great-grandmother Charlotte Ebury would have called *dinatoire*. We were Edwardian in our simplicity, our frocks were made in the village, our faces were polished with soap, we were incurious about the facts of life. It was hoped, but not insisted on, that at Les Marroniers we might acquire some French dress sense.

It was an old stone house with a mansard roof and a good deal of wrought-iron about it, shaded by a great chestnut tree. We slept in airy rooms with beeswaxed floors. Our fortnightly treat was a visit to the tiny Opera House of Vieux Colombes, like a tuppence-coloured Pollock theatre. There we heard all the light opera that never seems to be done nowadays—*Véronique, La Fille du Regiment, Le Jongleur de Notre Dame, Manon, Lakmé*.

In the Portland Place days it was no unusual thing for Hilaire Belloc to come to breakfast. He always ate two boiled eggs and impressed on me, aged about six, the absolute necessity of making a cross at the bottom of your egg when you came to it. His sister, the novelist, Marie Belloc-Lowndes, stout and rumpled and kind, my grandmother's dearest friend, was the only one of my elders to whom I did not have to excuse myself for wanting to be an actress, she knew about the ache to get out of one's environment, had felt it even in the enchanted surroundings of her home at La Celle St Cloud. Re-reading her two books[8] about this lost domain of youth I am at once transported back to the safe tree-shaded lanes of the charming shabby *quartier* of Vieux Colombes, now demolished.

The Aunts and my grandmother were going to win. My Scottish relations would have been satisfied for me to take a university degree and pursue some useful work; my father's sister had not married and had been her father's right hand in his Glasgow congregation. I had, however, been brought up with the idea of marriage perpetually put before me; the London Season loomed as a Public School loomed for my brothers, a different form of inescapable discipline. It was not likely to be pleasant but might be exciting. Scotland had been our favourite holiday place, even the contrast of strict Presbyterian Sundays was bearable as long as they did not go on for ever, but London, whose very syllables have deep

[8] *I too, have lived in Arcadia* and *Where Love and Friendship dwelt.*

and sombre reverberations, was to be my choice, though to me London never seemed like a capital city, rather it was a series of country estates lived in and in part owned by my relations.

I think with love of those family houses in London, my grandmother Caroline's in Mayfair, Aunt Blanche's in Victoria, Aunt Sophie's in Chelsea, Aunt Margaret's in Regent's Park, Aunt Katherine's in Pimlico, (hers the stately Governor's House of the Royal Hospital), and how one had only to turn up on one of these doorsteps to be hugged and exclaimed over by friendly servants, combed, and generally made presentable before approaching the drawing-room where the Great-Aunts had their being—dwelling like enchantresses in jewelled caves where objects, fragile and extraordinary, were duplicated in mirrors crowned with gold pagodas, and where jars higher than a child's head, restless with dragons and hunting Chinamen, stood about a peril to clumsiness.

The wide family kinship they shared rooted them in history and tradition. Tides of taste and fashion ebbed about them, but the roots held. I smile to think how amazed they would have been to hear their possessions discussed and valued by those whose mentality is of the sale-room.

One of the many disadvantages of being young was having all those adult eyes trained on one for family traits and tricks of likeness. The Aunts, whose own hair was thin and dry and worn piled up with an Alexandra fringe, took it upon themselves ceaselessly to criticise our hair. Our looks were, in a mysterious way (mysterious to us), their property. We were part of the family inheritance destined (by them) to carry on a tradition. Once daughters and granddaughters had married Mansions, with parks, picture galleries, pleasances, statues, and had effortlessly produced great statesmen and great hostesses and they were bountifully hospitable and concerned themselves with the keep and employment of a host of poor relations. By now the mansions were thinner on the ground (the poor relations too). 'He will, at least, have the family place,' would be said of some young man with nothing else to recommend him, as if the possession of a rural seat which he could not afford to live in must confer a virtue. I have heard my grandmother, enlightened on every other subject, say: 'I don't like Blank's politics *or* his manners, but I believe his elder brother is an invalid and not likely to marry now.' The disgraceful inference hung in the air, but I understood it. The long love-affair with inheritance had been going on for centuries, declining, reviving, never quite dying out. When I was with those dear enchantresses I was able to see it as the background of their humane and dignified lives devoted to caring for the poor at their gates (in my grandmother's case, since she had no gates, being a Londoner, for the Hospital for Incurables at Putney), and would find myself agreeing weakly that some dull girl (a modern Charlotte Lucas) *might* be right to marry for the sake of an establishment, she plainly being unfitted to keep herself by any other means.

This social world that moved between London and the country was really a very small affair, kept tight and secure by inter-marriage. The life-style of the late Victorian upper-classes, with a few glaring exceptions (but so few as to be unimportant except to point a moral), was based on a humanitarian outlook. It is often argued that, if there had been no abject poverty, *Bleak House* could not have been written, that for Dickens the poor were an inescapable necessity to set off the grace of charity. It is certainly true to say that for there to be a life-style such as that of my forebears there had to be strict obligations, the call for self-denial, the practice of paternalism interpreted in the most literal sense of the word.

Seeming to be so Olympian my grandmother and great aunts made their own mythology, backed by hospitable houses, kindly old servants, charitable projects, cast-iron political certainties, easy-going husbands, and a good deal of money.

When we were children they talked over our heads, mysteriously, in schoolroom French which servants were not supposed to under-stand. An example (delivered with perfect certainty that it would be understood), could run: 'Everyone knew that it was a *ménage à trois, en éffet un secret de Polichinelle*—one child at least was of the mist, *mais en même temps* accepted everywhere as *parfaitement comme il faut*—in Paris *bien répandu. C'est juste à dire* that the husband was *une bête féroce, il s'enrageait à folie,* etc. etc.'

They were above fashion as I have said; musically dogmatic, they venerated Bach and Beethoven as institutions, as they did the Anglican Church, tolerated Wagner because he was a German, worshipped Brahms and Chopin. They went to the Private View Day of the Royal Academy to look at portraits of their acquain-tances but not to buy pictures, of which they would reasonably have argued they had plenty already. Hand-made lace trimmed their garments, sachets of Elang-Elang were sewn to their corsets, they did not dull their exquisite complexions with cosmetics. They must have had exceptionally high standards about health for I never remember them not exchanging anxious whispers, carefully shielded from our ears, about 'symptoms'. They really loved their servants, treating them with the helpless leniency they showed to their horrid pets. They were endlessly, unimaginatively, ready to advise; and, imaginatively, just as ready to help where a present of money could put things right.

My grandmother Caroline was thought Bohemian, by virtue of being an artist and a writer. She had, they all had, the Wortley habit of staring (they were all myopic) which alarmed strangers; but no young person in need of a deeply concerned, unshockable, audience was ever not given the whole of her attention, her blue eyes behind the gold-rimmed pince-nez that made red marks on each side of her elegant nose would blaze with interest. On the whole happy marriages rather bored her; she liked to be told of the marital difficulties of the younger generation, particularly those her sisters were not yet aware of.

Aunts cannot be mentioned without mention being made of great uncles. Of Uncle Charlie, so specially dear, I have already written. Uncle Reggie Talbot scented his white moustache with Eau de Portugal, his linen was glassily white, he had princely manners to the young and his was the nicest of all the family butlers, Mr Fripp. Uncle Fred Firebrace, who married Blanche Stuart Wortley, was just a soldierly presence during holiday visits to their villa in Sussex, where a lawn merged without a break into a field of moon daisies. After Fred died, Blanche went to live in London in a tall house near Victoria Station filled with flowers that came up in hampers from the country twice a week. We stayed with this beloved great-aunt often during the Summer Session of Parliament; she slept very little and would be found by late returners from the House or from a party, sitting up in bed in a pink shawl reading Byron, having had a welsh rarebit for her supper. 'I would not,' she declared, 'exchange with the Queen!'

It was Aunt Katherine Lyttleton's husband, dear jolly Uncle Neville, who had the best touch with children. He came of a family of twelve church-going, cricket-playing Lyttletons,[9] but he

---

[9] The children of George, Lord Lyttleton.

was not so 'churchy' as the others. Katherine (the youngest of the girls of James's) got to work on him early. By the time I began to focus on them, Neville had been Governor of the Royal Hospital, Chelsea, for nearly fifteen years. He had been a soldier of considerable distinction; Katherine, however, had very little liking for moving about the world, she wanted to settle near her sisters, so, by convincing the War Office with a persuasiveness all her own, she installed him in the perfect Wren Governor's House where he was to remain until his death.

We, the children of the family, loved him. He found in me another Dickens lover and would quote whole pages to me. I never minded if he forgot and repeated himself. He enjoyed teasing Aunt Katherine by pretending to be 'just a simple soldier'. In fact he had been a brilliant Latin scholar at Eton, translating, at sight, what other boys took hours to prepare. He loved to make jokes, always the same ones; after a meal he would say: 'I feel better now—felt pretty good before.'

'I'm a fine fellow, aint I?' he would say, dressed to review the Pensioners on Oakapple Day, when the statue of the Hospital's founder, Charles II, is wreathed in oak leaves. My favourite memory of him is, when, with a stiff breeze blowing up the river and ruffling the white plumes in his cocked hat, he stands upright, his portly figure held in by the scarlet uniform of a Major-General, while, slightly staggering to imitate the tread of their younger days but indomitably upright, the old men process before him— veterans of the Zulu Wars, of Tel-el-Kebir, even the Crimea. He would not admit to finding them touching and said it was the wind that was making his eyes water.

Their three beautiful daughters with the pretty names of Hilda, Lucy and Hermione, were my mother's dear cousins, and life as lived at the Governor's house was something out of time. The house, one of Wren's minor masterpieces, was, and has remained, one of the loved houses of my life. My bedroom there had white eighteenth century panelling, it, and a lift and a housekeepers' room, had been carved out of one handsome saloon. There was a print of Le Camargo, flower wreathed, her feet set eternally in a dancing position; just across the lawns was the river, and all night long the hooting of barges and tugs went on. In love, I would lie wakeful hearing this friendly sound. Sheltered from fear I had grown up very slowly. Now I covered more ground, like a sapling that seems never to be going to make any growth until it is noticed that its branches have begun to cast a frail shade.

On one subject I was adamant, in spite of earthquake tremors from Scotland ('Sooner would I see her *hearsed* at my feet!'). I did not feel adamantine at all. I only knew that I must at least *learn* to act. My mother, with sublime moral courage faced the drawn-down upper lips and raised eyebrows of her relations, accepted that I would probably now never marry and might even sink to nameless depths, found me respectable lodgings in London with an indigent friend of a friend, and paid my first term's fees at the Royal Academy of Dramatic Art.

I had by now done more than one London Season. Very few of us enjoyed the experience, several of my contemporaries wrote mordantly in novels about it, one or two married in their first or second Seasons and spoilt the market for the rest. When I call back those London summers (my father was by then in the House of Commons and each year we left Elsfield for the Summer Session), I recall only the thump of saxophones in another house, the telephone that did not ring. The young men we danced with have faded from memory, and all of the houses in which the dances were held are gone—among them Londonderry House with Wyatt's great double staircase hung with Waterloo and Peninsula portraits, the first house in which I was to eat off gold plate. (The tree was dying at the top, but not visibly, not yet.)

The last party given in Dorchester House, Vulliamy's Italianate villa of the 1850s, was not grand but shabby, for the house had already been sold and on the Ballroom walls there were darker crimson patches where the Holford collection of paintings had hung. This did not trouble those who were lightheartedly living in the moment, treading the pavements as if they were daisy fields, leaf-shadows glancing across skimpy silk frocks (no one would have thought of calling them dresses). I thought once of writing a novel called *Leaves through a London Fan-light* because in Kensington and Camden Hill most houses had fanlights through which leaves growing in the Square outside could be seen, sharply green, making the narrow halls darker; tense with the feeling that Spring had only to come to depart again, with an after-taste of something missed.

It seems to me that through the mid-Thirties all London drawing-rooms were painted apple green, and hung with Thornton's

Temple of Flora prints. The worldly ones smelt of Floris' *parfum à bruler*. All dances were alike in detail, with striped awnings, sad little parcels of quails in aspic, drooping flowers sent up that morning from the 'place' in the country, a thump-thump of dance music, sometimes, but all too seldom, the one face longed and looked for, and in the street unemployed families looking for a bench to sleep on; we would wander outdoors with our partners on balmy nights and engage these in conversation. Once the Lovelaces lent Wentworth House[10] for a cousin's coming-out dance. The night was warm with a cool river breeze, the water catching lamp-light in swirls of oily gold. The Apothecaries Garden was opened for us; scented shrubs breathed heavily out on the night air. The seats all along the parapets of the Embankment had recumbent figures huddled on them—did any memory of the crossing-sweeper of my childhood come back to me then? I fear not. In love one is hampered by having to carry that awkward burden, that inner lamp that a breath can make glow or extinguish altogether, turning it, shielding it, as a woman carries a child, close. The lamp shines through the flesh and people say 'how well she is looking'.

[10] Their London house on the Embankment.

9

The Reasonable Shore

Life at Elsfield went on very much the same as it had been doing since our childhood. By the time I was in my teens I had gathered courage to disagree with my father's literary judgements. Pornography and the Irish were regarded by him with equal distaste (the poetry of Yeats and A.E. excepted). So, fighting for emancipation, I smuggled in *Ulysses*; it lived in a dust jacket of *The Pilgrim's Progress*, not unapt, and bravely I insisted on reading to him undigested lumps of Wyndham Lewis and Ezra Pound in defence of my right to be different. *Ulysses* being *Irish pornography*, the combination would have been altogether too much for him! Against the bias of his upbringing he admired Turgeniev and Dostoevsky, Balzac, Flaubert, and Stendhal. He was a natural critic like Bagehot, who he in some ways resembled. In the light of his devotion to the seventeenth century poets I persuaded him to read Eliot. D. H. Lawrence would not have been permitted reading for me, though I read him.

He had the Edwardian penchant for literary facetiousness: for Kipling's light verse, for Belloc and Saki, Somerville and Martin Ross, Beerbohm and Chesterton and Calverley; these he would read aloud to us in the evenings. Dining at Elsfield could be a punitive experience for shy undergraduates because of the literary games at which we excelled—having had much practice. But after-dinner readings of a new chapter of his latest book were memorable—to many unforgettable.

I imagine that few, if any, children of today would embark on the works of Walter Scott printed as they were in small type, and without illustrations to enliven the text. Yet read them I did. I daresay I skipped—or my parents bowdlerised as they read aloud. Yet stumbling, mis-reading words, making guesses at the incomprehensible dialect, I somehow got—or was got—through the great novels so that the very sight of them in a shelf warms my heart to this day. I treasure many passages, long ago learnt by heart, such as Flora MacIvor's contemptuous word-portrait of Edward Waverley:

'I will tell you where he will be at home, my dear,' she says to
Rose Bradwardine, 'and in his place—in the quiet circle of domestic happiness, lettered indolence, and elegant enjoyment, of
Waverley Honour. And he will refit the old library in the most
exquisite Gothic taste, and garnish its shelves with the rarest and
most valuable volumes; and he will draw plans and landscapes,
and write verses, and rear temples and grottoes . . . and he will be
a happy man.' And the old woman's rebuke to the rich spoiled girl
at a dying woman's bedside: 'Stand out o' my gate, my leddy, if
sae be ye are a leddy; there is little use in the likes of you when there
is death in the pot.' And from *Wandering Willie's Tale* the
description of Claverhouse in Hell: 'And there was Claverhouse,
as beautiful as when he lived, with his long dark curled locks
streaming over his laced buff coat, and his left hand always on his
right spule-blade[1] to hide the wound that the silver bullet had
made.' My father's rendering of the Lowland tongue would
make such music of these passages.

There cannot be a record of my youth that does not mention
Sir Henry Newbolt. The name immediately calls back to me the
Elsfield library, the hearth-rug trampled and rucked by the feet of
undergraduates, the armchairs sagging invitingly, with over our
heads a portrait of Raleigh looking out and away to other horizons:
a scene still held dear by men and women to whom it was part of
their Oxford years. In my mind he stands before the fire, hands
under his coat tails, rocking on his heels, waiting for a pause in
the talk into which to launch himself. To Lawrence Whistler who
married his granddaughter, himself a poet, Henry Newbolt was
the 'poet of honour', but I think he was more than that. He and
my father met during the War in the then Ministry of Information.
After 1918 Henry Newbolt was at a loose end looking for an
editorship in which his experience as a critic and writer and his
enthusiasm for the teaching of English would be of value; he
found it on the educational side of Nelson's, the small Edinburgh
publishing firm into which my father had gone as a working
partner before his marriage (having first learnt the basic techniques
of paper making and typesetting), and to which he returned after
the War. It was the beginning of a lifetime's friendship.

This meant reciprocal visits to Elsfield by the Newbolts and by

---

[1] Spule, spulzie = ravening for spoil, murderous.

us to Netherhampton, their house in Wiltshire. I remember singing folk songs at one of Lady Newbolt's village fêtes one hot July
when the limes were all in flower. (I was encouraged in this sort
of showing off, and it shames me to think of it.) Margaret Newbolt
had been a Duckworth of Orchardleigh, that fairy-tale Somerset-
shire house with a church on an island in the middle of a lake to
which Henry and she had been rowed to be married. By the time
I remember her, her total deafness made everything she said in
her sweet voice (so few of the deaf have sweet voices) sound
distantly wise, as if it came from somewhere beyond the chiming
of hours. Here were people in whose presence I did not feel all
thumbs and wispy hair. During Netherhampton evenings Henry
took turns with my father at reading poetry; my dear father's
choice often being the *Chasseur Noir* of Victor Hugo or the *Nuit
de Décembre* of de Musset, declaimed in French in a voice kept
specially for French poetry. It made us children giggle.

During a Kentish summer soon after 1918 my mother opened
a door for me on Keats. It must have been a hot summer, for I
remember that my feet were brown except for where the straps of
my sandals crossed over. There, for the first time she recited Keats'
Ode to a Nightingale to me, just as I was falling asleep. Hay-
making then was not done by combine tractors; the grass was mown
with scythes and swept into haycocks. We ate our strawberries in
the tree shadow, while out in the sun women in long dresses and
faded lilac sunbonnets rhythmically scythed with the apparent
effortlessness that is the result of long practice. The scene could
just as well have been taking place during the Napoleonic Wars
or in a novel of Thomas Hardy's. They were nothing to me, and
I, in a pinafore and a floppy linen hat drinking ginger beer gone
gassy in the heat, was nothing to them, yet for the term of my
mortal life I shall remember the scything women when these
words come back to comfort me for life's let-downs :

> Tis not through envy of thy happy lot
> But being too happy in thy happiness,
> That thou, light-winged dryad of the trees,
> In some melodious plot
> Of beechen green and shadows numberless
> Singest of summer in full-throated ease.

Now that I was beginning to develop a critical sense Henry

F

Newbolt taught me to look for what in Keats is spare and sinewy:
'You won't,' he said, 'though you now think you will, always prefer
the bits in *St. Agnes Eve* about the dia*mon*ded panes of quaint
device, in that context dragged in to rhyme with "carven imag'ries"
which they don't, or "jellies soother than the creamy curd", which
is nonsense because a jelly is one thing and junket another, but you
will not forget the description of the lovers creeping down the
stairs and how—

> A chain-drooped lamp was flickering by each door;
> The arras rich with horseman, hawk, and hound,
> Fluttered in the beseiging winds uproar;
> And the long carpets rose along the gusty floor.'

Indeed in the many cold houses I have lived in the image of those
carpets has often returned to me forcibly.

He encouraged my rather starved ego by writing me verses;
when I became engaged to a Lucy of Charlecote in Warwickshire
he told me that my new name would make me more than ever a
child of poetry, begged that I would revisit the garden of *The
Nightjar* (his favourite among his verses) at Netherhampton. Alas,
I never did.[2] It was odd how physically alike he and my father
were, though Henry was the taller. Walter de la Mare has written
how a remark that interested Henry would 'at once decoy the lean

[2] In a letter to me when I was just grown up he sent these verses:

> Now, dear child, when childhood ends
> Comes the time to weed your friends.
> Not, of course, that they'll be told
> They're too ugly, dull, and old;
> Half must go in any case
> Helter-skelter into space
> That the rest, the happier few,
> Still may walk and talk with you.
>
> Then may this old house be heard
> Haply, if it breathe a word;
> If it beg, since here you were
> As beloved as you were fair,
> That you'll revisit it at times
> With its old walks and lawns and limes,
> Its old people, her and him, –
> Till their memories grow dim,
> And you too are moving west,
> Far from any last year's nest.

clear-cut Roman face in your direction, alert as a kestrel'. The bust in bronze of my father, now in the National Portrait Gallery, has a strong look of Julius Caesar—in some moods he could look like Cromwell and, as we often unfairly told him, behave like him.

As a week-end daughter I would have to subdue my suspicions that the politicians who sought my father's company were crooks, fast-talking manipulators and social climbers, like Brendan Bracken and 'Prof' Lindemann, who I now discover to have been not nearly so old as I always thought him—he talked in a voice that creaked like an unoiled door, was yellow in colour from the peculiar diet he lived on, and haggard from the snubs he had to take from the smart High Lifers whose company he sought.

Oxford in the early Thirties was more political than arty—the Twenties had been the great age of the aesthetes. Quintin Hogg, Evelyn Baring, Frank Pakenham, Alan Lennox-Boyd, Basil Ava, Edward Stanley, all made their individual impact; to my father who had been an Oxford contemporary of Basil's uncle, Basil Blackwood, it appeared that these were the Jasons, and would win the Fleece. He was never more outgiving than when talking to undergraduates who brought back to him his own Oxford. Laughter would be spontaneous, the young men would take away a sense of having been given a glimpse that would ever after colour their memories of their Oxford days.

My father was first and last a historian, and historians of an older generation were among the most frequent and most welcomed visitors to Elsfield; Gilbert Murray, who had been his classical tutor at Glasgow University with his wife, kind Lady Mary, who others thought formidable but who did not intimidate us, and the historian George Trevelyan whose daughter Mary then up at Somerville was my father's goddaughter.

George Macaulay Trevelyan let it be known that he wanted no posthumous praise. I would not wish to incur the malison of one I so revered, but perhaps in the Elysian fields where he walks with Acton and Froude, he will give a nod permitting the child, who on country rambles at Elsfield had so much ado to keep up with his long stride, to express her thanks. Like my father he was an insatiable walker, looking stern and abstracted the while. I did not often see him smile, and his laugh was rusty from, perhaps, disuse. Yet benevolence wonderfully softened his expression when he was among friends. I see him striding along the Roman Wall

toward Housesteads which he gave to the nation, under the windy
Northumbrian skies that were his birthright, his eyes bright, his
old-fashioned ulster flapping. And because of him I am enabled
to see it, not just as a low wall winding across moorland, but as a
continuous Citadel fortified against invasion. To him the frontier
of the Then and Now was thin, and this was his gift to me.

I must here record, with regret that I never knew him better,
another of my father's friends, a small weathered fellow-Scot,
W. P. Ker.[3] During a party at All Souls' to which I had been
taken under protest and was sulking, he got me away on the pre-
text of showing me how the Astrolabe in the Codrington Library
worked. But what he wanted me to see was not the progress of the
planets but a plant coming up between the stones of one of the
smaller quads. 'Smell a leaf of this,' he said. 'It is musk. As far as
I know it is the last plant of musk to be found in England which
still has the scent with which Elizabethan ladies made themselves
irresistible.' Later Cosmo Lang[4] at a party at Lambeth showed me
a painting hanging beside the fireplace of a girl with red hair
against a sea-green background. 'She was Penelope Rich,' he said,
'Sir Philip Sidney's sweet poison.' I stared entranced at the pale
little face of a woman poets had gone mad about. Did she, I
wondered, use musk for her witchery?

Toward a Christ Church undergraduate, a shy Cornishman,
whose militant political views were totally opposed to my father's,
yet who, as he would be the first to admit, was softened and won
over by the openness of Elsfield's welcome and the talk he heard
there (no historian who does not deal in facts alone can be a
revolutionary for long), my parents felt a special warmth. His
continued friendship meant much to my mother in her widow-
hood; evenings at Elsfield were repaid by him with presents of his
books as they came out and affectionate letters that went far toward
mitigating the loneliness of her last years. Among the tributes to
him that were published after my father's death there was none
more heartfelt than that of A. L. Rowse, remembering times past
and the long thoughts of youth. 'History,' he said, 'is not the rival
of the Classics or of modern literature, or of the political sciences.
It is rather the house in which they all dwell. It is the cement that

[3] Fellow of All Souls. Oxford Professor of Poetry.
[4] Archbishop of Canterbury. As Bishop of Stepney he had performed
my parents' wedding ceremony.

holds together all the studies relating to the nature and achievement of man'.

By now I was in London, a student at RADA, whose Principal,
Kenneth Barnes, had been an Oxford contemporary of my father,
also a member of the Oxford University Dramatic Society—
not surprising since all the Buchans can act. I now had other
friends, and with them set up a very different London, roaming murky byways not dreamed of in my younger forays, not
among City churches but among way-out shabby old Music Halls,
eating in restaurants that preserved an Edwardian style—the Café
Royal, not redecorated since Max Beerbohm's heyday, Gatti's,
Monico's. Many a rag was had by us at the Troc and the Cri, in
company which included a future Poet Laureate. These were the
days of the Jarrow Marchers, of Hitler and the Anschluss, of Ellen
Wilkinson trumpeting about the English aristocracy: 'We don't
guillotine 'em now, we tax 'em.' Warnings were in the air but we
hardly heard them.

There should be at every stage of life moments of pure cogni-
tion, as Henry Newbolt wrote in a letter to me, when one stops
dead in one's tracks and shouts aloud, '*Now* is the time of my life!'
Sadly it does not work like that. Or not for me. I seem never not
to have looked before and after and sighed for what was not.
Others have lived through the best of times and the worst of times,
have seen the Horn of Plenty emptied yet declared, like the Queen
of Bohemia, 'I am still of my wild humour to be as merry as I can
in spite of fortune.' That kind of compensatory gaiety I never had
except in selected company. Mercury, who rules the Gemelli (my
masters) and is the lord of language, is a volatile but not a dancing
star.

A crippling love affair had made me wary. Half consciously I
was looking for someone to marry who would be Scottish enough
to pacify Gran, who would be liked by our old servants, approved
by my brothers, a countryman but not obsessive about it since my
roots were in London (they were to turn out to be shallow ones).
So powerful was my heredity that I fear I made a private reserva-
tion that it would be nice if he were to come into a 'place', but not
quite at once. The summer of a dormouse was nearly over; brash
as this sounds I knew I could be happy and useful somewhere, I
did not as yet know where.

When I met a man who fulfilled some of these qualifications—

who was a soldier with Highland forebears, who had seen the world as I had not, who was the second surviving son of a rather run-down family that had lived on the same piece of Warwickshire for eight hundred years but was perfectly prepared to live anywhere I chose, and who was besides infinitely charming, good-tempered, generous, readily amused—Reader, I married him!

A rented house on the edge of the Cotswolds was to be our first real home. It was for its size spacious. It had a shallow valley at its back with walnut trees. We were hard up but wages were not high and we afforded horses and a groom who stayed with us till he died. Fred Messer came from a nearby village, one of a long descended family of Liberal-voting, good-living country men and women, and spent his winter evenings (there was no pub in that backward village) reading Dickens. He brought our two children up to have a proper respect for craftsmanship and to enjoy and use their daylight hours, teaching them gentle manners with animals and people according to his own strict standards.

Our furnishings were sparse but life was cheaper then and decent wine could be bought for seven shillings a bottle. We were not too far from Oxford for my brothers to bring their friends to dine on summer evenings on our small lawn in front of the gracefully proportioned house with its pillared porch.

How can one write of a long marriage that weathered so many changes as mine did, with the inevitable eroding hour by hour of the sands? Only to say that the dramas of wrecks and sunken rocks are spaced at long and longer intervals, until in the end the tide comes in to fill the reasonable shore.

I do not think it ever occurred to any of us four children that the fixed planet, whose benign influence like a pull of gravity kept us circling within its orbit, would be extinguished. The outbreak of War in 1939 was less dreadful in its impact for us (after all we had known it was coming) than our father's unexpected death in 1940 at the age of sixty-four. Too short a life for all he had in mind to do. He had set Cromwell and Montrose, Sir Walter and Augustus Caesar, in just perspective in a steady meridional light. Abhorring violence, he had written of demonic possession, brawls, stabbings, diabolism, intrigue; one day in the far future when he had killed off his fictional heroes he meant to be free of his public

who ravenously called for more. Having ignored ill-health all his
life, he did not expect to die; nothing I am sure was further from
his mind. But what *was* in his mind? I think he wanted in the last
stage of his life to have time to call back the memory of the
Oxford friends whom he never ceased to miss, to walk the Peeblesshire hills in the company of the two brothers he had lost. But
until that day arrived he meant to work for his country, and
Canada[5] taught him much that would be valuable in British
political life. He wrote to me in the month before he died asking
me to put my mind to the problem of making Elsfield a much
more labour-saving house, perhaps pulling down the Victorian
addition and turning it back into the small manor house it had
been in Dr Johnson's day. I detected in his last letters a wish to
get to know me much better now that my three brothers would be
going to the War from which they might not return.

In his busy middle age he had tended to pigeon-hole us in his
mind, only looking a little sad when we refused to stay in our
holes, though always ready to accept the reason why (we hated to
disappoint him, he praised so wholeheartedly whenever he could).
That there was a whole area of experience we could not share
with him had to be accepted. I was sometimes asked : 'How did he
find *time* for you all? In his full stretched life there must have
been somebody who went to the wall.' At this distance I am not
sure of the answer. It probably works out for the best for fathers
not to have too much time for their children, I am not convinced
of the value of parental interference. His Presbyterianism came to
be worn more lightly as he grew older and moved away from his
mother's rigid conformism, like an old coat comfortable to resume,
with affectionate recognition of the quality and durability of its
cloth.

He worked with the beat of a machine, taut with the effort not
to betray the pain he more or less always suffered. A friend has
written of how, arriving a little late for an appointment, she found
him lightly sleeping, and that, when woken, all his faculties sprang
immediately into action, as might a knight's who has lain down
under a tree to rest a moment, but not relaxed his grip on his
sword. (In the days after his death when the whole western world
joined in mourning him, there went through my mind over and

[5] My father accepted the appointment of Governor-General of Canada
in 1935, and died there in 1940 of a cerebral thrombosis.

over again the ballad couplet, '*I'll lay me down to bleed awhile and then I'll rise and fight again.*')

His career has been told and has passed into history. He himself as I have said, was small and spare with a bird's watchful blue eye. An American critic has written of the *culte* of friendship and of understatement, 'which, until lately, have shaped the most coherent and truly civilized of modern political communities, that of Britain', and of the ideals of that understatement 'which the scruples of a supremely confident *élite* imposed on its members'. The *culte* of friendship had been Oxford's gift to my father; his spare beautiful prose style derived from his commitment to the Classics.

I found for him a quotation from the etymologist Fabre about the Noctuids, the night moths, for whom *the dark is light enough* and he seized on it for it seemed to establish another frontier. He often experienced when walking alone on the moors an intimation of the power of the lonely hills (as Wordsworth did) that would send him headlong in search of running water or grazing sheep, in medical language called *agoraphobia*, defined no more clearly today by the medical profession than when the Greeks coined the word. Frontiers like this can be stumbled on unawares, passing a point 'no more than a line, a thread, a sheet of glass', that divide the here-and-now from the unknowable. He believed that the Dead need to recuperate from the pain of living for aeons beyond mortal comprehension and thought it wrong that this peace should be invaded by clumsy human attempts to drag them back. He was absolute for death, and both life and death were thereby made for him the sweeter.

Nothing that I could say about him would reveal him as do his own writings in which a fresh imagination fed by loving curiosity speaks from a mind to which despair was alien. The parallel with Scott is felt. Both had been voluminous authors and in their writing had striven to unsettle no man's faith, nor written a line that they would wish to see blotted out—Sir Walter's words.

A critic[6] of our time rebuked a young would-be critic who had scoffed at Thackeray; pointing out that 'to have written beautifully; to have preserved faith in goodness in spite of observing that it is usually speckled; to have consumed your own smoke instead of

[6] Desmond Macarthy.

blowing black depression in other people's faces; to have refused to regard yourself as a great exceptional man though half the world proclaimed you to be one; to have been naturally generous and reckless and yet steered yourself prudently and sheltered those you loved; to have lived honourably after this fashion and to have written so that those who came after can still see life as you saw it; this is an achievement which should exempt a writer at any rate from the patronage of inexperience.' It all too seldom does. It did not exempt my father from the petulant sniping of lesser minds.

Within thirteen years of each other my mother's aunts and my grandmother died, the men of the family had long preceded them. The houses in Mayfair, Victoria, Pimlico, Chelsea went. The family ties held together by the hands that had steered our youthful destinies, slackened once all these hospitable roofs were gone. Of cousinly warmth in my own generation there was plenty, we were delighted to see each other when occasion presented itself but it presented itself less and less often. We were much poorer, we had to have jobs, or worked ourselves to a standstill running servantless houses, growing food, raising families.

After the War our lives, my brothers' and mine, diverged; the centre could not hold. Elsfield was sold for a fraction of its value as Moor Park had been after 1918. The library too was sold—I minded this. Susan moved into a dark house in a village with a strip of garden where before she had looked over a landscape to the sun setting forty miles away. We were changing. We needed to concentrate on our children, it was for us to try to recreate for them something of the old custom and ceremony we had inherited as a bulwark against the future. My brothers came back from the War with a strong will to recover and to found their own *foyers*. This was achieved, and it was good. With gentle irony our father nicknamed his two elder children, John and me, the Greeks, the two younger, William and Alastair, the Barbarians. It was apt. We two elders were now content to conform, the younger ones with greater originality and ambition went their own distinctive ways.

What can I write of the youngest of us, the one who is gone, Alastair, the visionary, the interpreter of history? It has recently been said of him that he had 'that combination of intellect and compassion known as wisdom (that) motivated the great contribution he made to scholarship and to a generation's understanding of the

F*

transformation of international relationships.'[7] This is the cumbrous language of official recognition; more simply Alastair Buchan was a citizen of the whole Western world and was as much a Canadian by marriage and an American by spiritual adoption as he was an Englishman by birth and north country by descent. The years between us contracted as we both grew older. He had written sadly after our father died that could he but hear again the timbre of that beloved voice it would fill his sails as with a fresh wind from the sea. If I could but once more hear *his* voice it would feel to me like a following wind at my back.

In his book on Walter Bagehot[8] he revealed himself. Alastair wrote of Bagehot that: 'the balance he achieved by superhuman effort had been won by victories in a private campaign against himself, against arrogance, against intellectual pride and folly, against circumstance, against dejection and ill-health.'

The wearying tussle with ill-health and attendant depression that furrowed his face and folded a perpetual frown there alarmed some people but not for long. Behind it there welled a pure spring of compassion.

To his father John, the eldest of my three brothers was the embodiment of a dream and none of the rest of us resented it. He has been a great traveller, and in his manner, distant yet kindly, gives the impression of one who halts momentarily to bend all his attention to a problem that presses but whose mind is on the next lap of the journey.

Humans like to believe that there is in them a quirk of singularity, something out of step with the times they live in which in another period in history would have given scope. It is often more obvious to an observer. I see Alastair in the Parliament of 1781 during Lord North's unlucky administration, at the high moment when Charles James Fox's motion for terminating the war with the American colonies by peaceful settlement has been defeated, his height making him formidable as he leaps up to catch the Speaker's eye to express profound disapprobation.

My brother John I see spending the evening of his life in Italy in a gash of the wind-grieved Apennine; I picture him, his travels being over—'*heureux qui comme Ulysse a fait un beau voyage*'—

[7] The words are those of his friend Dr Henry Kissinger, then USA Secretary of State.
[8] *The Spare Chancellor*, a life of Walter Bagehot by Alastair Buchan.

in a library of sporting books, with heads of chamois, and a few large gentle dogs beside a fire of driftwood, compiling another beguiling volume of memories in which he combines his own philosophy with knowledge of country habits, and salts it with a gentle dry wit.[9] That he, in fact, has most of what I want for him on the northern shore he has chosen for his habitation, does not affect my picture of him which places him as a follower of Garibaldi in the Italy of 1859. I know that after his war experiences[10] he left a piece of his heart in Italy.

My brother William is easiest to define in terms of another century. His talent is to aerate any company in which he finds himself with bubbles of his individual essence. If either of them had ever permitted the other to get a word in edgeways, how happily he and his ancestor the Earl Bishop would have spent time planning vistas and approaches, over a bottle of Falernian wine and a *beccafici*. The time-slot that should certainly be his is the end of the 18th century, a period that had room in it to build palaces, sow barren rocks with clover, and indulge a taste for witty exchanges by candlelight.

Our father had published his first novel before he left Oxford. He had (and admitted it) the incalculable advantage of having been young and a writer at the beginning of this century when to be both was to have the ball at your feet, a time that was never to come again. By the late Thirties the war was upon us. William, a fighter pilot, was flung from all he loved and understood, to Ceylon and India. He had produced some youthful *jeux d'ésprit* already, but it took fierce loneliness sharpened by an acute eye and ear for the dying poetry of Imperial India, to produce his first novel which contains his best writing.[11]

Though born a Londoner, after 1945 I opted for a country life with husband and children in the Cotswold country, at a half-way point between Oxfordshire where my mother was living and Charlecote in Warwickshire, my husband's family home in which

[9] *Always a Countryman* and *One Man's Happiness* by Lord Tweedsmuir.
[10] In 1944 he was with his regiment of Canadians on the Plain of Lombardy close to the ancient city of Ravenna, the last seat of the Roman Emperors, the buttress of our right flank on the sea. Byron had ridden and Garibaldi hidden in the pinewoods there.
[11] *Kumari* by William Buchan.

I now write, soon to become a property of the National Trust.

Gloucestershire was still as unspoiled as when W. R. Lethaby[12] wrote of it fifty years earlier: – 'in many a tiny village, set there out of the rough winds and driving snows of winter, were to be found marvellous stone-built farms, their steeply gabled fronts making a lovely brightness in among the dark woodlands, or bringing the long grassy slopes of the limestone hills to a sharp finish with their picket ends against the sky'.

When we went to live in the valley of the Gloucestershire Coln in a plain stone house built in the 17th century (in living memory it had been a working mill), Daneway and Pinbury, houses in which Gimson and Barnsley had designed and made furniture, were in other hands, those of our friends—the Laureate Jan Masefield at Pinbury, the architect Oliver Hill at Daneway. Our nearest neighbours were David Talbot Rice, the historian of Byzantium and his dynamic and beautiful Russian wife, Tamara; further off, at Oakridge, lived William Rothenstein, the painter—to be the close and much missed friend of my middle years.

Kelmscott, too, was not far away. I have wandered round sleepy Lechlade wondering which was the shop where Janey bought the children's sunbonnets, and the carpenter's yard where Dante Gabriel went for book-shelves and an ebonised cabinet in which he kept her photographs. And pictured the coffin on a farm cart, a plain wreath of laurel on it which the rain made glisten, in which Morris, the angry, lonely man, who never condescended or gave quarter to faulty work, was carried to lie in Kelmscott churchyard.

In this valley there were still working mills. One, a mile or so up the river from us, let down its brown flood daily between the thick banks of meadow-sweet and ragged-robin that folded in our stretch of the Coln, as it had been doing since Domesday. For nearly two hundred years the plain, serviceable fashion of our mill house, its dormers added as the miller's family increased, had stayed the same, the huge tie-beams that held up the ceilings were scored and dented by the mill's ratchet wheel and pulleys. When two rooms were made into one by us, the separating wall, when stripped of its plaster, was found to be chalked with the weights and prices of grain of nearly a century earlier.

Einstein had said that if we could actually see any happenings

[12] *Ernest Gimson, his life and work* by W. R. Lethaby, 1924.

in history they would be the size of a postage stamp, perhaps smaller; looking back, I see, like one of F. L. Griggs's marginal drawings, *le dessein, c'est la probité de l'art*, the curve of the river as it flowed past our windows, two Irish yews defining the scale of the sturdy stone house that sheltered our children's childhood.

In my own childhood I observed, without understanding what I saw, a world which is gone beyond recall. I like to think that I remember Henry James who was its chronicler, though I suspect that, with adult hindsight, the wish may be father to the thought; certainly there *was* an elderly gentleman in a creased silk suit, exuding a strong aversion to small children, on the terrace at Ockham among pink and green parasols, with the (by me) loathed white cockatoo sidling round the tea-table, nipping ankles. His letters to my grandmother are all about week-end arrangements and might have been written by anyone. I had been so hoping for some Jamesian circumlocution on the subject of trains;—'those, if one may so express it, iron arbiters of our lives inhumanly in-different to the desire that sends us journeying, a desire in no way diminished let me assure you, dear lady, by the prospect of an hour's wait at York, etc.'

Only the middle-aged read Henry James, I think; no one has written more acutely than he did about the English country house before its decline, even when glazing his observation with archa-isms, as—'It is always on the mild children of the glebe that the complex superstructure rests.' He was not so in love with it all as not to perceive that the relationship, based on feudal dependency, of landlord and tenant, master and servant, was deeply flawed and would eventually be doomed. His imagined houses that have lattice-windows with broad cushioned seats, looking out on fault-less lawns and curious topiary, are, even as we re-read, fading with the passions, disciplined and austere, of his characters as the picture of the terrace at Ockham fades and grows small and distant in my memory.

There comes a time to be done with re-reading letters which tug at the heart. Some letters to my mother I held in my hand for a long time before I burnt them, recalling the painful articulation of the man who dictated them, in the grip of a progressive illness that paralysed him. Already blind, he would soon be speechless. The room he lay in was high up in a building in New York's 84th Street. Once when passing through New York I went to see him to carry him my parents' greetings. To be invited by Edward Sheldon was almost a royal command so I took trouble about my appearance, forgetting that he could not see me. In his sight-immobilised presence I felt ashamed. He knew exactly what I was feeling and put me at my ease by asking what colours I wore.

Edward Sheldon had been a playwright and though an invalid was still an influential man of the theatre.[13] I was young and hungry and ate ravenously the delicious meal he provided for his guests, while he guessing my addiction talked huskily of plays and the great players he had known. The allotted hour was gone in a moment. Afterwards he dictated this to me—'You won't always go on looking and sounding like the young Ellen Terry,' (he could not know how I looked). 'In fact you may have to deprive yourself of the only form of self-expression you believe in, but if you can write down what you feel you have got the drop on them all.' After my son was born in Oxford, (on the night when all its bells were rung for the end of hostilities, May 5th, 1945) a domestic event of which he could not have known, he sent me a telegram from across half the world : 'I am thinking of your father'. It was his valediction to me.

The West or garden door of Charlecote opens onto a river terrace. Across the river is a view of what in Shakespeare's day was called The Great Meadow. Tonight a thin mist is rising from the water. I am not tempted to linger on the terrace steps. I go in and close the shutters with a heavy iron bar put up after a burglary in 1850. Because its air does not move, my room seems warm after the river damps. It has subtly changed its character since the lamps were lit. The family portraits retire into their heavy foliated frames, the Poussin (genuine or no) becomes a black cave in which figures of Antiquity gesticulate in the meaningless manner of their kind. The fire in the white marble hearth needs stirring up. What an invitation to the resources of scissors and paste, the choosing, discarding, piecing, snipping! But by now my self-imposed task is done.

[13] His play *Romance* was one of those run-away theatrical successes of the pre-war era that defy explanation, creaking and old-fashioned as it would now seem. It should be due for revival. The plays of Harley Granville-Barker, another family friend to whom I owe infinite thanks for his kindness to me when a drama student, have endured and are being rediscovered.

The men and women who move through this book, move away, diminishing figures in a huge landscape, trailing their elongated shadows. One last glimpse of my great-great-grandmother, the first Lady Wharncliffe, completes the cycle which began with her as a child at the Evian breakfast party of 1786.

Harriet Granville, whose letters cover the politically eventful years from 1810 to her husband's death in 1846, had always had a fondness for her. Herself a shrewd, observant, faintly embittered woman, obliged as the wife of a diplomat to dissemble, she loved Caroline for being like cool moonlight after an airless day. In April 1844 she wrote to her sister, Lady Carlisle: 'I see I have not said enough about the Drawing Room. The Queen bowed and smiled and hoped I was well, but less gracious than Prince Albert who seemed inclined to embrace me. Leopold careworn, absent, Kent civil. Very few people. Lady Wharncliffe, entirely enclosed in a gold frame-work, just like the barley-sugar *treillage* one sometimes sees over cream and strawberries in an *entremets,* a great love, in ecstasies over the darling cream-coloured horses. Lady Jersey, a very good-natured old woman, the Duke of Wellington in radiant health and spirits. Ouf! dearest sissie, it bores me as much as being there to fight it over again.'

Thus lightly she foretells the Victorian Court to come with the Queen learning to control her natural impulsiveness, growing becomingly plump, obsessively enamoured of Albert who is perhaps finding the company of sophisticated older women as restful as Byron had found Lady Melbourne's, the old Duke lit by the last flare-up of a sinking candle, Lady Jersey, once the Regent's mistress, now a well-painted old woman, content to be spiteful no longer. The Court entertainments not quite so insipid as they had been under Queen Adelaide when the King had tried to teach Caroline how to play Commerce, but for Lady Granville they were a wearisome repetition of many like occasions. Lady Wharncliffe in her barley-sugar gown would be cheerfully ready to be amused, the Doge, now Lord Privy Seal, would be gravely attentive to Prince Albert's plans for the domestic reorganisation of the royal palaces, he was deeply interested in problems of drainage and heating.

Wortley receded from the family scene a long while ago. My mother and her cousins remembered how they loved having the London train stopped for them at a Halt and being lifted down and carried to the waiting barouche for the drive to the house. By the end of the century the house had been enlarged with another wing and a tower, by now blackened by the smoke of the Wharncliffe Collieries. As D. H. Lawrence wrote of an imagined house in the same situation, 'smuts fall and blacken the stucco that has long ceased to be golden.'

Moor Park was sold. My mother, after going back there for a valedictory visit, wrote: 'A statue of Neptune, brown with age, with a pitcher in his hand from which water trickled, sat comfortably gazing in front of him, half engulfed in a Portugal Laurel whose embrace became more urgent as time went on. I parted the branches and looked at him as he sat, entirely hidden. My grownup years rolled away for a moment as I gazed down at a basin full of brown water, stiff dead laurel leaves and wriggling tadpoles. It was just the same as ever.'

But not for much longer. Developers were already eyeing the undulations of the park, the perfect turf of the lawns, the trees that would have to be uprooted in order not to impede the fairways, anticipating the tinkle of ice in glasses at the bar that would be set up in the White Saloon.

This quiet room and the mood of the moment incline me to try and hear before they fade the voices that are only a bat-squeak, or the whine of a wet finger rubbed round the rim of a wine-glass. The voice of an ancestress across more than two centuries—'life to be endurable should not be considered too near'—of a young girl in revolt against the idea of a suitable marriage, 'there are certain *ignis fatuis* that frequent these marshes rank, riches, diamonds, carriages . . .'—of a non-conformer satiated with luxury, 'the intense glory of the place depresses me . . .'—of a newly-made wife about her young husband, 'I think he took but one step from the chaise into the room.'

The voices fade and I shall not try to call them back now that the black tin boxes have received back their contents for another generation to assess. The mansions that were family homes are experiencing a new usefulness. Ockham was burnt down, it is believed in the village that Aunt Mamie returned from beyond the grave with this intention, in order that no vague middle-class heathens should inhabit it after her.

Our grandchildren, hopefully, not being travellers in time as we have been, living between two worlds, will be able to be coolly critical rather than subjective. No one rooted in the mid-nineteenth century as my grandmother and great-aunts were, and to some degree my mother, and having received traditions and precepts from those whose parents were born in the eighteenth century, could be expected to foresee the gulf that would inevitably yawn between them and myself. With love and good faith they enclosed my childhood and shaped my future in a sort of vacuum of non-belonging. All that I, the inheritor, have been able to do, is to write down these *recherches*, from the hearsay, half heard, half understood, of childhood, and the memories, actual, but already receding into the mists of time, that are counterparts of the old scrap screens in that they have no focal point but only a mass of detail, chosen at random, now dim with age and the ill-usage of the nursery.

The Stuart Wortleys of Wortley Hall, Sheffield

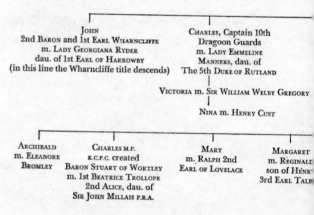

JOHN
2nd BARON and 1st EARL WHARNCLIFFE
m. LADY GEORGIANA RYDER
dau. of 1st EARL OF HARROWBY
(in this line the Wharncliffe title descends)

CHARLES, Captain 10th
Dragoon Guards
m. LADY EMMELINE
MANNERS, daü. of
The 5th DUKE OF RUTLAND

VICTORIA m. SIR WILLIAM WELBY GREGORY

NINA m. HENRY CUST

ARCHIBALD
m. ELEANORE
BROMLEY

CHARLES M.P.
K.C.P.C. created
BARON STUART OF WORTLEY
m. 1st BEATRICE TROLLOPE
2nd ALICE, dau. of
SIR JOHN MILLAIS P.R.A.

MARY
m. RALPH 2nd
EARL OF LOVELACE

MARGARET
m. REGINALD
son of HENRY
3rd EARL TALBOT